What Others Are Sayin

MW01058112

The Gospel is the good news that in Christ Jesus, God is reconciling all things to Himself, that He is ever restoring every broken thing, and that He is dispensing grace and peace as far as the curse is found. The Dominion Mandate is simply the call to graciously manifest this glorious good news in every area of life. In this helpful new book, David Bostrom powerfully echoes that call for a whole new generation of believers. I gratefully recommend it.

George Grant
Pastor, Parish Presbyterian Church

David has created a serious antidote for the under productive, unmotivated modern Christian. I don't know of a better hands-on guide for the common man to unleash the calling God has given him. When every man as priest successfully contributes his gifts in God's community, then we will ignite the light for the world to live by.

Calvin Jones
Concert/Recording Pianist, Soundtrack Producer

Who are you? What is your purpose in life? How are you supposed to live and carry out your calling? Where worldly philosophers fail, *Get Dominion* outlines the answers to these questions. It shows how to stop being a spectator of life and participate in bringing about God's will on earth as it is in heaven. Buy this book, read it to your family, and tell your friends about it!

Buddy Hanson, President
Grace & Law Christian Worldview Resources Center

David Bostrom offers the sincere and practical Christian a clear and well-marked path through a no man's land filled with theological landmines. Dodging the mines, he takes the reader's hand and leads him in Biblical simplicity to obedience in love. Well done!

The Rev. Franklin Sanders
Rector, Christ Our Hope RE Church

While most books on dominion are rich in doctrine, David Bostrom's new book gives extremely practical suggestions for day to day living to apply the biblical command to take dominion in all areas of life. First, he gives knowledge, then understanding, and finishes with wisdom for all ages and walks of life. It is well rounded and well balanced. I wish someone had given me a book like this when I was beginning to walk with God. In one book David has distilled down values and beliefs and practical suggestions that I want my children to have for their lives. It will shorten your learning curve by 15-20 years.

Todd Robinson, M.D.
Robinson Family Clinic

I fear that the declaration "Jesus is Lord" has become nothing more than a mere platitude to many modern Christians. David Bostrom attacks this problem by forcing us to face the practical implications of this glorious reality. What does the fact that Jesus is Lord mean for you? How are you submitting to His Lordship in your life? How will you honor His Lordship in the future? David confronts us with questions essential to living lives that glorify the Lord Jesus—and that makes *Get Dominion* vital reading for every Christian.

Pastor Steve Wilkins
Auburn Avenue Presbyterian Church

David Bostrom's book, *Get Dominion*, is a must read for every Christian! His practical no nonsense approach to discovering your God given destiny is both challenging and inspirational. Don't underestimate your worth to Christ's Kingdom, read this book and start living the life you've dreamed of today!

Jay and Laura Laffoon
Celebrate Your Marriage

David has underlined the fact that the Dominion Mandate and Great Commission apply to all believers. With the power and the prompting of God's Spirit within, every believer's Biblical assignment is to live all of life to the glory of God, reaching out to whomever crosses our path—whether in the workplace, at home, or at play. The old expression, "full-time Christian service," usually assigned to only some, actually applies to all believers in every facet of life—and life's clock is ticking!

Charles Thor, Jr., Senior Vice President (retired)
Jewel Companies, Inc.

The Dominion Mandate is God's call upon our lives to gardenize, make beautiful, and bring all things under the authority of Jesus Christ. In his book *Get Dominion*, David Bostrom gives us a compelling account of where our ambition and purpose need to be. I've heard David teach these concepts for years, and I'm delighted the truths he has to share can now reach a larger audience. This book will help you live the life God intends for you!

John Pollion, President
General Housing Corporation

The title says it all. . . "Get Dominion." This is a practical book regarding God's call on our lives and how we are to go about fulfilling it. In *Get Dominion* you will not only find insight about escaping the world's perspective of what life means, but wisdom concerning how embracing God's call provides focus, meaning and freedom to fulfill your created purpose. These truths are foundational for the Church to impact the culture and are the positive anecdote to our political representatives failed mortgaging of our future. This book is a big gift in a small package. It teaches and motivates in a way that is simple and effective. Open it and use it.

Bill Garaway
President, Kuyper Media

David Bostrom shows us the Dominion Mandate is about creating value for others and in his insightful writing he has created great value for each of us. David presents truth in a simple, straightforward manner that is inspiring, challenging and, at times, convicting. Utilizing the power and truth of the Dominion Mandate, David skillfully takes us on a journey of discovery that clarifies important concepts like "freedom," "work," and "spirituality." This book moves beyond practical instruction and presents purposeful application that can empower us to transform our lives, equip us to impact the world, and enlighten us to realize our Kingdom purpose.

Lyle Wells
President, Integrus Leadership

GET DOMINION

You've Been Called to Fulfill a Mission

DAVID BOSTROM

Foreword by R.C. Sproul, Jr.

Disclaimer: *Get Dominion* provides practical ideas concerning the application of the Bible to all of life. No guarantees are made that you will achieve any particular results from the information presented.

Published by David Bostrom
DOMINION MANDATE MARKETING

www.madefordominion.com
info@madefordominion.com

ISBN-13: 978-1478383567
ISBN-10: 1478383569

Printed in the United States of America

Dedication

This book is dedicated to all who want to be as faithful and fruitful as possible with the gifts they've been given.

The book is also dedicated to my sons—Jonathan, Paul, Jordan, Daniel, Andrew, and Matthew—who have been called to get dominion.

Acknowledgments

I'll tell you upfront, there's not a lot of original material in this book. What's here is largely a collection of ideas I've absorbed from brighter lights over the years. Without men like Jay Adams, Gary DeMar, George Grant, James Jordan, Bill Mouser, Gary North, R.J. Rushdoony, Franklin Sanders, Andrew Sandlin, R.C. Sproul, Jr., Steve Wilkins and Douglas Wilson, this book would not have been written. Not by me, anyway.

My goal in writing is simple. Take some profound ideas and present them in an understandable format so the lives of those who read them would be changed. This book is not written for theological heavyweights, though I believe they would benefit from the material. The readers I have in mind are ordinary people who know there is more to life than they are experiencing, but can't put their finger on what they're missing.

There are several others I would like to acknowledge who contributed to the book. I'd like to thank Dan Kennedy, who more than once said, "You need to write a book." I'd also like to thank my friends Bill Garaway, Joe Marsh, and Mark Mehling who gave valuable help in the publication process. I'm grateful as well to my wife, who has always been my number one editor. And, I want to say thanks to my friends at St. Stephen's, who have provided me a quiet place to write.

It's also fitting that I express my gratitude to Burke Shade and John Pollion, two friends who have consistently gone out of their way to be an encouragement to me. And, of course, I'm grateful for both my parents and in-laws, who have been a constant source of love and support.

Most of all, I want to thank Jesus Christ for redeeming my life and giving me many reasons to live.

Contents

Foreword

R.C. Sproul, Jr.

Vanity of vanities, all is vanity, said the wisest man to ever live. So he began the book of Ecclesiastes.

There King Solomon set about to find meaning. He sought meaning in his labors, and failed. He sought meaning in wealth, and failed. He sought meaning in the pursuit of pleasure, and failed. He sought meaning in the accumulation of wisdom, and there too, he failed. It mattered not where 'under the sun' he sought for meaning, because the hard truth is life 'under the sun' would always make shipwreck of his quest.

Solomon was not asking if life is itself meaningless. Rather he was asking, if there is nothing that transcends us, and if all there is to life is the here and the now, then what is our purpose? Whatever basket or baskets in which we put our eggs will be smashed on the immovable reality that we will one day die. Death destroys purpose, if this world is all there is.

Solomon, of course, knew we do not live our lives strictly under the sun. There is a transcendent realm, a transcendent God, and therefore a transcendent purpose. But as Solomon pretended the trail ended at death, too often we live as though it actually does. We think there's no connection between here and eternity, and therefore all that matters is eternity, and here, well, it's neither here nor there.

Too often we determine all that matters is our invisible souls, and the souls of others. This is what will last forever. And our labors, the food we eat, the roofs we put over our heads, the institutions we build, those are just necessary evils. We look at our work as just a tool to make the money to pay the bills to stay alive so we can prepare for when we are dead. This too is vanity.

If our lives never cross the border from the temporal to the eternal, either because there is no eternal, or because you can't get there from here, we are indeed but players who strut and fret our hour upon the stage. If this life never touches the next life, life is indeed a tale told by an idiot, full of sound and fury, signifying nothing.

My friend David Bostrom, however, reminds us that this is not our circumstance. He reminds us not only is there a transcendent realm, and a transcendent purpose, but that these are intimately tied to our life, our work here.

He does not blaze the trail between the two worlds, but points us along the path the Lord Jesus trod before us. In focusing on God's original and abiding call on our lives, that we would fulfill the Dominion Mandate, that we would be fruitful and multiply, filling the earth and subduing it, all under the Lordship of Jesus Christ, we find that our days are not vain, but are overflowing with meaning and significance, that our labors enter and reshape eternity, that our cups overflow.

Along the way David, who has been gifted with the spirit of Barnabas, encourages us to not lose sight of the forest for the trees, nor the trees for the forest. He encourages us to see the forest in the trees, and the trees in the forest. He gives practical counsel on how we can and should understand our abiding call to fulfill the Dominion Mandate. He provides wisdom by which we can not only work with purpose, but with integrity, and passion for the glory of Jesus Christ.

This work gives us eyes to see that we are not doomed to live our lives under the sun, but are blessed to live our lives under the Son. It in turn reminds us of the wisdom the wisest man I've ever met always tells me, "Right now counts forever."

Introduction

"Where there is no vision, the people perish. . ."
~ Proverbs 29:18 (KJV)

Are you having a hard time figuring out where you fit in this world? Are you frustrated because your efforts don't seem to have the significance you think they ought to have? Do you know deep down there's more to life than what you're experiencing, but can't seem to get a handle on what it is? Does a lack of vision for your life make you feel like you're dying inside?

If your answer to any of these questions is "yes," then this book is for you.

> Are you having a hard time figuring out where you fit in this world?

And you are not alone. There are countless people today who struggle to discover what their lives are about. Sensing something's missing, they spend their days searching instead of living. After a while, most give up the search. When this happens, it's ruinous to the soul.

In the best cases, those who give up the search resign themselves to a life of boredom and depression. They get through life the best they can by occupying themselves with the many diversions this world offers. In the worst cases, it can mean a life of anger and resentment. And this usually leads to behavior that's destructive to oneself and others.

We see the fruit of this all around us. It doesn't matter if we're talking about a person who fills his emptiness with one amusement after another or one who loses his cool because he hates what his life has become. We're talking about the same thing—a life without purpose.

Vision

The core of this problem is a lack of vision and understanding about why we exist.

When you don't have the big picture of what you're here for, and how the parts fit into the whole, futility sets in. You lack energy and drive to go after a better life, and disillusionment results. When a lot of people are at this point, whole nations are vulnerable. And without a turnaround, they perish.

But there's good news. Getting a vision for your life is not something you have to contrive on your own. It's been revealed. You just need to discover it, and apply it to your situation.

To make this discovery—and find your purpose—you need to see the story of your life in light of the larger account of what God is doing in the world, and the purpose He has for humanity.

We can find our place in this story in the very first chapter of the Bible. Genesis chapter one is well-known for its account of creation. What's much less known is this same chapter gives us the foundation for what we're to be doing in this life.

The Dominion Mandate

This foundation has been called the Dominion Mandate, and it's what this book is about. I've written what I have here so you not only know what the Dominion Mandate is, but can apply it to your life. That way you can identify your life's purpose and live it out.

It's unfortunate so little has been written about how the Dominion Mandate applies to us today. I believe it holds the key to finding your life's mission. Once you understand the mission God has for the world, and the mandate He has given you, discovering your purpose becomes more straightforward.

For over 20 years I served as a pastor. During that time, I did what pastors normally do—I preached, taught, married, buried, counseled, and so on. I found all these duties rewarding in their own way. But my greatest satisfaction came from helping others realize their place in God's world. In order to help those in my care see this, I regularly found myself explaining the Dominion Mandate.

We need to rediscover the Dominion Mandate in our time. Individuals need it to find their way in our complex world, and nations need it for their very survival. If we really want to know what God wants for our lives, learning the Dominion Mandate is a must.

The Middle Ages gives us the inspiring story of how Irish monks preserved the treasured knowledge of their day while civilization collapsed around them. They were able to do this because they were grounded in the Dominion Mandate. They knew God had work for them that transcended their own time. And, because of their commitment to that work, they provided a bridge to the next stage of civilization.

There's a Place for You
We also live in a time when the foundations of civilization are being destroyed. But the earliest foundation of them

all, God's Dominion Mandate, still stands. And no matter who you are this mandate applies to you.

God has a place for you in this world. He's authorized you to fulfill a mission. A mission that's significant. By coming to understand the Dominion Mandate, and how it applies to your life, you can find your purpose.

I've written this book so your life would be improved by reading it. But this should not be regarded as a typical self-help book. It's different. It will challenge you to consider the biggest issues of your life. Even more, it will lead you to look to God as the only one who can provide you with the purpose and fulfillment you're looking for.

The book is divided into two parts. The first part has to do with foundational truths. Here, I present the worldview necessary for you to understand the world and find your place in it. The second part shows you what you must do to apply what you've learned and experience the purpose God has for your life.

I've provided Scripture references after some sentences so you can investigate further how the Bible has informed my thinking.

It is my pleasure to present this work to you.

We've ALL got a mission to fulfill. And MY mission is to help YOU discover and implement yours.

PART ONE

FOUNDATIONAL TRUTHS

Chapter 1

We Have a Mandate to Fulfill

You Have to Know God's Purpose to Figure Out Your Own

"And God blessed them, and God said to them, "Be fruitful and multiply, and fill the earth and subdue it; and have dominion over the fish of the sea and over the birds of the air and over every living thing that moves upon the earth."
~ Genesis 1:28

Every year legendary Green Bay Packer coach Vince Lombardi made a practice of taking his team back to "first principles." As the team would gather for its first preseason meeting, Lombardi would walk to the front of the room with a football in hand. Then, after a dramatic pause, he would hold up the ball and say, "Gentlemen, this is a football."

What was the point of this ritual? It was Coach Lombardi's way of drawing his team back to the fundamentals of the game. He knew it was only as his team remained clear on the basics that it would be able to fulfill its mission to win football games.

What Lombardi did for the Green Bay Packers, you need

to do in your own life. You have to make sure you are constantly clear on the basics. You need to know what your purpose for being here is. To get that clarity, you need to look at the Dominion Mandate revealed in the Bible's first chapter. It's here God gives us our most basic assignment in life, and commissions us to get busy fulfilling it.

What Lombardi did for the Green Bay Packers, you need to do in your own life.

The Scriptural foundation for the Dominion Mandate is quoted above. When you look at the words of this text, several basic truths stand out. These truths serve as a starting point for our consideration of the Dominion Mandate. So let's consider them.

The Dominion Mandate is About Being Productive in the World

While many people today are caught up in consumerism, God created us to have a different focus. He made us to be producers. He designed us to be co-creators, who develop and serve according to the gifts He has granted each of us. And it's in this we find purpose in our activities.

When we think of God's charge to be productive in light of the words "be fruitful and multiply," the obvious implication is there ought to be children. This seems straightforward, but in our current environment it calls for some emphasis.

Columnist Pat Buchanan has pointed out that due to lower birthrates and abortion, the U.S. work force is shrinking at the same time the number of dependent adults is growing. This imbalance will put an enormous strain on the economy. Both the aging population and those trying to support it will suffer.

This fact shows us that as much as we may find children to be inconvenient, we need them. Of course, there are other reasons to have children, but those reasons lie outside of my point here. That point is simple: without children, civilizations die.

But the call to be fruitful and multiply goes beyond producing children. It involves being productive in other areas—like developing land, growing food, constructing homes, harnessing energy, and starting businesses of all kinds. That's because the Dominion Mandate is about creating value for others by developing and expanding what God has already given us. And doing it in every area of life.

> The call to be fruitful and multiply goes beyond producing children.

There's much discussion today about diminishing resources and everyone getting his fair share. From the perspective of the Dominion Mandate, these issues need not be a problem—if our focus is on bringing forth, enlarging, and making plentiful as God calls us to.

Although people don't often verbalize it, they do recognize the value of production. This is why those who are most productive are generally better paid. This is as it ought to be. Those who produce get rewarded.

But when people don't produce, they plunder from others who have. And this is one of today's problems that must be reversed.

The Dominion Mandate is About Taming and Developing Creation

It might be hard to imagine when you look out your window, but there was a time when there was nothing but wilderness. The only way this wilderness was pushed back was the first humans began to tame what was under their care, and those who came afterward applied themselves to the same task. Eventually, small sections of the globe didn't look so wild anymore. This process led to the development of civilizations.

Today, we still must subdue what's under our care. Just let a garden go for a week and see how wild it starts to look. The garden doesn't tend to itself. It needs the constant maintenance and care of a human being. The approach we must take toward a garden is what's to occur in every area of life. We need to bring what's in our care under control in order to get dominion.

Some will argue we ought to let nature run its course, and claim that the call to subdue and get dominion is oppressive. But let's remember the nature of the mandate. Bringing the earth into submission is what God has told us to do. It's the way He has devised the whole earth to be developed. This does not mean we're to carelessly exploit the environment. But we are to care for and manage whatever is our responsibility.

Some years back my neighbor across the street had a serious ground mole problem. The moles' tunnels were so plentiful they forced the upheaval of his entire front yard. I decided to go offer my neighbor some help. When I approached him, he thanked me but explained he believed in "live and let live" and was going to just leave the moles alone. I couldn't persuade him otherwise. But, you can be sure once those moles tunneled their way under the street to my yard, I took care of them. I had to. It was part of taking dominion.

14

The Dominion Mandate is about more than just filling the earth. It has to do with conquering and taming it. It involves overcoming the earth's resistance and making it fit for the fullest development possible.

The Dominion Mandate is About Bringing God's Rule to All That He Has Made

When people think of rulers these days, it isn't usually with much fondness. And no wonder, every day we're used to finding corruption and self-serving attitudes in the rulers we're exposed to. But take note: there isn't anything inherently evil about being a ruler. We know this because God has commissioned us to rule.

To rule has to do with exercising power over what's under your authority or control. It involves governing and guiding for a particular purpose. This purpose can be for good or evil. And, of course, God calls us to rule over our particular domains for good. He has given us a kingly role over His creation. We are to serve as viceroys under His authority. We are to further His realm in the particular domains He has called us to.

The domain of the first man was a garden. The task God gave him was to cultivate and keep the garden (Gen. 2:15). Soon after, others were learning to rule over their own portions of the earth. Some ruled over livestock and others metal. All of this involved learning and skill development. As understanding increased, so did the ability to rule effectively. And this ability has accumulated from one generation to the next.

Today, this process continues. We increase in knowledge, and we apply what we know to our areas of expertise. We implement what we develop, and we pass it on to future generations. It's in this way the Dominion Mandate is extended through all honorable occupations and lays the groundwork for those who come after us.

The rule that the Dominion Mandate calls us to is comprehensive. It involves a stewardship over all of creation. Even the fish of the sea and the birds of the sky are included. In this mandate you are to find your purpose as you busy yourself with whatever God has given you to do.

Whenever you struggle with your purpose in life, go back and ponder the words of the commission God gave us in Genesis 1:28. In them you'll find the foundation for a meaningful life.

The Mandate Encompasses All of Life
There is no area of existence that does not fall under God's commission to us. It doesn't matter what area of life we talk about. God entrusted it to our supervision. Once you realize this, and grasp the immensity of the task we've been given, the world looks like a much different place.

First, there's no longer the dualistic idea that there are some areas of life God is interested in and others He leaves to us. The earth is the Lord's and all that is in it (Psalm 24:1). Because it all belongs to Him, He has an interest in it all. True, some areas of life have more important functions than others. But everything in life has its place before God.

Second, the comprehensive nature of the Dominion Mandate brings sanctity to your everyday activities. Even the smallest task or most obscure station in life has significance. Washing dishes, changing a diaper, digging a hole, going to the dentist, entering data, traveling for business, and thousands of other mundane activities take on a whole new meaning once you embrace the Dominion Mandate.

Third, the world becomes a bigger and grander place. Without the Dominion Mandate, the world is just a place where we pursue our own small agendas. But with the Dominion Mandate as our foundation, the world becomes the arena where God's purpose for humanity extends itself. It becomes the locale where His magnificent story continues to unfold. A story of which we are a part.

When you catch a glimpse of the all-encompassing nature of this mandate, hope rises. You are able to see life isn't just an endless cycle of weeks and years punctuated by fun times and crises. It's the medium God uses to work out His grand plan through history.

Abraham Kuyper was an amazing man, and you ought to know something about him. Kuyper was a pastor, journalist, and statesman. In 1901 he became the prime minister of his homeland, the Netherlands, and served in that capacity for four years.

Kuyper was extraordinarily gifted. Few could match his achievements—in his day or our own. But Kuyper had a view of life that can—and should—be adopted by us all. Kuyper saw God's rule pertaining to every issue in life. This conviction was so strong it drove him to apply God's Word to all of society, which was extremely secular at the time. Though He faced stiff resistance, Kuyper's efforts blessed his generation.

Abraham Kuyper's view of reality is summed up in his well-known quote:

"There is not a square inch in the whole domain of our human existence over which Christ, who is Sovereign over all, does not cry: 'Mine!'"

There's a Domain for Everyone

The Dominion Mandate extends to all humanity. It includes everyone. And for good reason. The commission God gave in this mandate is so massive it takes a multitude.

The Dominion Mandate has a common purpose shared by mankind. Together we're to subdue and develop the world for Him, with each individual having his or her part.

The Bible describes the idea of each individual having a role to play when it speaks of the Church as a body with many gifted parts (1 Cor. 12). Though the reference here is specifically about the Church, the idea extends further to life as a whole.

So, there is a unity and diversity at work in the Dominion Mandate's fulfillment. Together we're to press on with a united purpose. But we do so by overseeing our own individual domains.

It's typical for people to think of the domain they have in terms of their vocations. Of course, the domains we have are really bigger than our paid work, but thinking of our vocations this way is helpful. People have considered their vocations as a realm to rule for a long time.

The Bible gives us many examples of people ruling over specific domains to further the overall dominion effort.

Jubal was the first who developed the area of music. He became the father of those who play the harp and flute. Abram labored in the field with flocks and herds, and developed skills for raising and multiplying livestock. Solomon worked with knowledge and ideas, and had as his main pursuit the furthering of wisdom. Paul's domain was the area of revealed religion, and upon this foundation he established churches.

The practice of having a particular vocational domain has continued through history. In early American history the realm a man covered was often revealed by his last name. Everyone knew what Mr. Smith did, or what occupied the Baker family. Today, we may not have people named Mr. Programmer or Ms. Web Designer, but the idea of having a vocational domain still exists.

But as mentioned, one's domain is not limited to vocation. There are other areas of life to manage, too. Your mind, body, spiritual life, relationships, family, talents and skills—even opportunities—are all under your charge and part of your domain. Really, anything for which you are responsible to care for in some way comes under the Dominion Mandate.

Once you realize you have your own domain, and it's linked to God's commission for world-wide dominion, how you approach your life takes on a greater seriousness. With it comes hope and meaning because you come to understand what you do matters. It's part of a much larger effort.

Made in God's Image

As you think about the Dominion Mandate, it's natural to wonder how we could be a part of such a mission at all. How is it possible for mere humans to take raw materials and concepts and develop them to become something of higher value than they were before?

The answer is we're made in God's image.

To be made in God's image is to be made in His likeness (Genesis 1:26). God created us different than Himself, but enough like Him to perform the work He called us to do. And when you combine this with the fact we were created from the dust of the earth, we seem specifically designed to rule over creation as God has ordered us to.

To understand what it means to be created in God's image, let's compare some of the attributes of God with the attributes we have as people.

God has certain eternal attributes that define His character. He is righteous, just, loving, merciful, all-knowing, all-powerful, immutable, eternal, and so on. For God, these attributes are infinite and perfect.

We reflect these same attributes. Our reflection of them is limited compared to God, but it definitely shows the likeness of the One who made us.

Why do we have an internal sense of right and wrong? Because we've been made in the image of the One who is perfect in righteousness. Why do we have the ability to love and be loved? Because the One whose image we bear is love. Why do we have the capacity for imagining, reasoning, and speaking as we do? Because we've been made in the likeness of God who has these abilities.

It's on the basis of these God-derived attributes we're able to pursue the Dominion Mandate. God hasn't just given us a mission. He's also equipped us to carry it out. **And as you pursue this mandate in the area God has called you, you serve as a co-creator with Him, amplifying what He has begun.**

The Mandate is Still in Force
I find it remarkable the Dominion Mandate is so often disregarded. What could explain this fundamental instruction from God being ignored as it is? Unbelief, false views of spirituality, unwillingness to engage the world, and faulty theologies that dismiss parts of the Bible all play a part.

But what really matters is not why the Dominion Mandate is overlooked. What matters is realizing it's still in force.

The Dominion Mandate remains God's charge to mankind. It has never been repealed. In fact, Christ's Great Commission to "make disciples of all nations" is a New Testament reiteration of the Dominion Mandate.

The Dominion Mandate continues to be the most basic direction God has given humanity.

The Bible begins in a garden, and it ends with the vision of a glorious city, the New Jerusalem. From generation to generation this vision is to be pursued as mankind fills and rules the earth. The mandate is fulfilled not by force, but through service according to God's Word.

Together, the Father, Son, and Holy Spirit call you to participate in the work of developing all creation. When you respond to this call faithfully, you fulfill your purpose and share in the glory of God.

If the Dominion Mandate is mentioned at all today, it's usually to introduce comments about our need to take care of the environment. Unfortunately, many of these comments end up elevating the creation above the Creator.

God must remain supreme in our care for the environment, and we honor Him as supreme by laboring as faithful stewards of the world He gave us.

Those faithful to the Dominion Mandate have no desire to trash the world with pollution or waste. Rather they seek to carefully preserve the world while in the process of developing and beautifying it.

> The Dominion Mandate remains
> God's charge to mankind.

Summary

- ◆ Fundamentals are always important. When times are tough, going back to them is even more important.

- ◆ The Dominion Mandate is the most fundamental assignment God gives us in life.

- ◆ The Dominion Mandate is about producing, developing, and ruling over the earth. In this way mankind continues what God started at creation, and does so under His authority.

- ◆ The Dominion Mandate applies to all of life. There is no area of existence that lies outside of God's attention.

- ◆ There is a unity and diversity at work in the Dominion Mandate. Together we share God's commission to rule over the earth, but we have different roles in bringing the commission to fulfillment.

- ◆ We are able to pursue the mandate God has given us because we are made in His image.

- ◆ The Dominion Mandate has never been repealed. It's still in force today.

Make it Personal

1. How does the Dominion Mandate's call to "be fruitful and multiply" apply to you?

2. What is under your responsibility that you need to tame and develop?

3. How does the call to rule over your domain cause you to view your life differently?

Chapter 2

Why the World is All Messed Up

There's a Reason for the Trouble We Face

*". . . as sin came into the world through one man
and death through sin, and so death spread
to all men because all sinned."*
~ Romans 5:12 (ESV)

When you recall the part you've played in any big project, you know how exciting it can be. The planning, designing, gathering resources, starting, anticipating, persevering, and finishing leads to the satisfaction of a job well-done. It gives a sense of exhilaration that makes you feel fully alive.

But I'm sure you've also been part of a project that left you sour. Who hasn't joined a committee or group project with high hopes of getting some worthy goal accomplished, only to be disillusioned by petty jealousies, fruitless arguments, broken commitments and abandoned efforts?

What's the explanation for this?

On the one hand mankind is capable of remarkable achievements. We are thrilled when a fellow human being makes a heroic rescue and marvel that we can have real time communication with a new acquaintance on the other side of the world. But at the same time, we grieve over the misuse of skills to cheat, hurt, and even destroy.

Where did the world go wrong?

Historians like to point out major events that mark a shift from one period to another. The fall of the Berlin wall, a relatively recent event, has been marked as the end of modern times and the beginning of postmodern times. Not everyone is aware of this.

But there is one event everybody needs to be aware of. Because even though it occurred many millennia ago, it explains so much about why the world is the way it is. That event is known as "the Fall" of mankind. And it's this event that gives us the biblical explanation as to why there is evil in the world.

The third chapter of Genesis tells us the first man, Adam, was told by God he could eat from any tree of the garden but one—the tree of the knowledge of good and evil. Soon after, Adam was tempted by the lie that eating the fruit from this forbidden tree would open his eyes and make him like God. He fell for the temptation, and because he served as a representative of the entire human race, we've been feeling the consequences ever since.

Adam's failure was essentially a matter of trust. God intended Adam—and all humanity after him—to fulfill the Dominion Mandate by trusting His Word. In this way progress would take place in God's own way and time. But Adam couldn't wait. He was impatient and immature. He grasped for what he thought belonged to him before its time.

As Adam's offspring, we share his impatience and immaturity. We also share the corruption that became part his character. None of us are as bad as we could be,

> Why is mankind capable of doing so much good, but at the same time inclined to produce an equal amount of evil?

but we are all tainted by sin in a way that twists our motives, thoughts, and actions.

This explains the world as it is today. Why is mankind capable of developing so much good, and at the same time inclined to produce an equal amount of evil? It's because the image of God in us has been corrupted by Adam's sin.

The fallen nature we share has a direct bearing on the Dominion Mandate. In short, it makes it more difficult. When you consider the following consequences of the Fall, it's not hard to understand why.

Death
God warned if Adam disobeyed Him he would die (Genesis 2:17). God kept His Word. When Adam sinned, the penalty followed. Adam did not experience physical death immediately. That came later. But Adam did die spiritually, as made clear by his desire to flee God's presence.

Death is a great enemy because it takes away life. But it also brings an end to the work of dominion. When you die, your efforts toward building God's kingdom are over. We are aware of this when someone who is outstanding in his or her field dies an early death, but it's true for everyone.

As Ecclesiastes puts it, once death comes, you can do no more. This is why you need to give your best while you can (Ecclesiastes 9:5-6, 10).

Man is Lost
The penalty of spiritual death causes us to be born into a state of being "lost." As the fellowship Adam originally had with God was broken, so is it broken with us. We all enter the world spiritually disconnected from our source of life and direction.

In this lost state the faculties for dominion remain intact. This means a person is still able to rule over his realm. But it will take place without God's purpose in mind. By God's common grace, human talent may still be used for good. But that same talent can be used to bring harm. A doctor, for example, may use his skill to save a life or abort it.

The state of being spiritually separated from God is the root cause of our misery as human beings. It's the reason mankind has lost its way when it comes to its meaning and purpose.

Blame Shifting
When God confronted Adam about his disobedience, he didn't own up to his responsibility. He denied being at fault, and blamed his wife instead.

We've inherited the same tendency. You can see this pattern in yourself whenever you deny responsibility for your wrong and blame someone or something else. This method of fault management does not need to be taught. It's there in our infancy. By adulthood, most of us have turned it into an art form.

One of the main ways we blame shift is by keeping double standards. We expect others to meet a higher standard than ourselves. Or, we demand others show us mercy while holding them to strict justice. In either case, we attempt to deflect responsibility from ourselves.

Blame shifting hinders the Dominion Mandate, because there's no way to fulfill your purpose without taking responsibility.

Thorns and Thistles

One of the ways God brought judgment for Adam's sin was to curse the ground. This was a fitting way for God to respond. Just as man rebelled against his Creator, now the creation rebels against man.

The curse as described in the Bible is agricultural. Instead of the land bringing forth desirable fruit, it now brings thorns and thistles (Genesis 3:17-18). But this curse goes far beyond agriculture. It includes all fields of endeavor. Why does so much of what we do seem so difficult when it should be so easy? It's because of the curse.

There is good news that comes with thorns and thistles. Since we don't like being afflicted by difficulties, these nuisances can cause us to turn to the Lord for His mercy.

Diminished Ability

Before the Fall there was an efficiency to human effort we no longer enjoy. This isn't just because the problem of thorns and thistles didn't exist. It's also because man operated at peak performance before the Fall, but doesn't anymore.

Adam's first task in ruling the earth was to name the animals. The Bible presents this task as being done quickly and easily. Adam could do this because he had optimal use of all his faculties. When he named the animals, his knowledge, imagination, recall, and mental clarity all functioned perfectly.

Not so with us. The Fall has diminished our abilities in a big way. We learn slowly. Our memory is weak. We have clouded thinking. Our imagination is twisted. And the knowledge we have is mingled with errors. This makes the work of dominion far more difficult than it would have been without the consequences of the Fall.

As I write, the news is abuzz about the latest mass shooting in the U.S. A young man walked into a theater and began firing at its occupants. The incident left at least 12 dead, and over 50 wounded.

There's a lot of speculation about why the shooter committed such a horrible deed. And, of course, there's been the predictable outcry about the availability of guns. But I have yet to see a story in the mainstream media about the real root of such a tragedy.

We like to pretend that we are all good people at heart. But the reality is we've been corrupted with a sinful nature. Without the grace of God, the capacity for evil deeds resides within us all. When a society such as ours denies this truth, acts of violence and wickedness increasingly become ordinary events.

Evil Within

Most people will admit evil is a reality. But there's disagreement when it comes to its source. Today, it's common to pin blame on certain inanimate objects—like guns or alcohol. Or on certain institutions, or political philosophies. It's thought if we can just rid the world of these, we'll have utopia.

But the real source of evil is hard to accept. It's within us.

Since Adam's fall, we've each become our own worst enemy. Our fiercest struggles come from within, because our hearts are a fountain of evil desires.

For the Dominion Mandate to be fulfilled, the corruption that lurks within us must be set right. But since the problem resides within us, we aren't capable of coming up with our own remedy. It can only come from the One who is able to remake us.

Disrupted Relationships

From the beginning it's been God's intent to have the entire population of the world cooperate to fulfill the Dominion Mandate. It's far too big of a task to be accomplished by anything less. So it makes sense for all those made in His image to work together in fulfilling His purpose.

But there's a problem. The Fall brought more than just division between man and God. It brought division between man and his neighbor, too. This makes it difficult to get even the smallest groups—even groups of only two people—to cooperate for any length of time.

Marriage conflicts, sibling rivalry, neighborhood disputes, church fights, business disagreements, crime, and war all show the disruption that the Fall has brought on our relationships. And whenever these disruptions occur, it impedes the Dominion Mandate from being fulfilled.

Guilt and Shame

When Adam sinned, his guilt and shame pushed him into hiding. As sons and daughters of Adam, we react the same way. And sadly, many of us spend our lives coping with our own guilt and shame instead of living out our purpose.

The Dominion Mandate is an outward endeavor. It

involves continually creating and increasing the value you bring to the world. It's about expending yourself and expanding your influence through the particular domain God entrusted to you. Guilt and shame make us timid, and drive us inward. Together, they cause you to see yourself as broken, and unable to cooperate with God's purpose until you're fixed.

Guilt and shame also mar our relationships with others. When we live under the shadow of these twins we're inclined to seek some form of atonement. We do this either by punishing others or punishing ourselves. With the one we want to destroy another's success. With the other we sabotage our own.

From Producer to Parasite
The first man and woman were to tend the garden so it would be fruitful. But the garden was just a starting point. As their productivity increased, their domain was to expand. And through the efforts of succeeding generations, the world was to be "gardenized."

But with the Fall we became disconnected from this purpose. We went from being producers to being parasites. The focus on doing the work God wanted done stopped. Human attention shifted to figure out ways to live off the labor of others as much as possible.

The consequence of this situation remains today. Laziness, which is completely contrary to the Dominion Mandate, is the most common example. But you can also see it as we accept economic systems that plunder the productive members of society for the sake of those who aren't. Unfortunately, we've grown so accustomed to this that many have difficulty seeing it at all.

Abuse and Abandonment
God gives men the authority to rule. The reason he gives

this authority is so men would use it responsibly to promote good and further the Dominion Mandate. But with the Fall, the act of ruling has been corrupted, driving those with authority in a couple of directions.

One direction is to abdicate responsibility. For example, when a father is negligent and inattentive to his role, he is abdicating. If a pastor is unwilling to take a faithful stand, he abdicates as well. If any of us remains silent when we should speak, we, too, abdicate.

The other direction the Fall drives rulers is toward abuse of their positions. If a business owner mistreats his employees for his own gain, he would be abusing his authority over them. The same can be said of civil rulers in a nation. We see the worst form of this kind of abuse in cruel dictators.

King David shows how a man can be guilty of both abusing and abandoning his role, in that he failed to lead in battle and took another man's wife for himself. Here he both abdicated and abused his authority.

In our day, the abuse and abandonment on the part of leaders has become so common virtually all leaders are viewed with suspicion. This, obviously, does not help the Dominion Mandate advance.

The consequences of the Fall make for a sad state of affairs. Instead of having a unified world seeking to fulfill the Dominion Mandate, we have a world hampered by sin's curse, leading to selfishness and division. The whole world suffers because of it. YOU suffer from it.

Yet God's intent for dominion has not gone away. His basic call to humanity is still to rule over the world and develop it for His glory. But He knows we can't do this in the state the Fall has put us, and that's why

He's intervened so we can.

Summary

◆ Human beings have the capacity for great accomplishment and unspeakable evil.

◆ The human capacity for evil comes from the fact the image of God in us has been corrupted by the first man, Adam, and his fall into sin.

◆ The following consequences of the Fall affect every one of us: we die, we are born lost, we blame shift, our work is afflicted by thorns and thistles, our abilities are diminished, we battle evil within, we have disrupted relationships, we experience guilt and shame, we're susceptible to live as parasites rather than producers, and we're inclined to abuse and abandon our authority.

◆ The whole world suffers because of the curse of the Fall. But the call to have dominion over the earth remains.

◆ For mankind to develop the world and rule over it for God's glory, we are dependent on His grace and intervention.

Make it Personal

1. How does understanding the source of evil in the world help you as you live your life?

2. Of the ten consequences of the Fall mentioned, which do you believe is having the most significant influence on your life at this time?

3. What can you do to overcome the effects of the Fall in your life?

Chapter 3

He's Making All Things New

There's Hope for Our Lost World After All

*"Of the increase of His government
and of peace there will be no end."*
~ Isaiah 9:7 (ESV)

To press on toward any objective you need reason to believe that objective can be achieved. You wouldn't think of pursuing a goal you were certain was impossible to reach. You would come up with a new plan to follow.

This raises an important question about the Dominion Mandate.

Is there any hope it can be achieved? The weight of sin on our world makes it seem impossible. But for the Dominion Mandate to give purpose for our lives, there has to be some prospect that God's original intent can be realized. If there's no hope it can, we'll have to find purpose somewhere else.

> God has instituted a plan of redemption so the work of dominion would continue on.

Well, good news. There is reason to follow the Dominion Mandate and find our purpose for life in it. God did not leave us to ourselves after the Fall. He instituted a plan of redemption so the work of dominion would continue.

God's Redeeming Grace

When Adam sinned, it set loose a chain of consequences. We observed ten of these consequences in the last chapter. But there are other consequences, too. Consequences that affect the whole cosmos.

First, God instituted a war between the seed of the woman and the seed of the serpent—a war that exists to this day. It is a battle between good and evil, truth and lies. It's a battle that rages behind the scenes of all that's taken place in history—and it lies behind all we face in our lives today.

But God also instituted something else. He instituted a plan to redeem the human race and restore it to its original purpose. By this action, God put us in a place where the Dominion Mandate can be pursued for the good of humanity and the glory of His name. God instituted this plan of redemption by His grace. And the plan is now in the process of being accomplished.

God's plan of redemption began when He provided a covering for Adam's guilt and shame, and in this way reclaimed him as His own. From Adam, God also preserved a godly line that would ultimately lead to One who would be anointed as the Savior of the world.

Through this line, God called a people for himself who were to be a blessing to all nations. The formation of this people began with the call of Abraham, and continued on through his descendants.

Over the course of centuries, those called by God's name

have shown both faithfulness and unbelief. At times, only a few faithful ones could be found, but despite the periods of infidelity, God remained faithful to provide a deliverer.

And in the fullness of time, God sent forth His Son, born of a woman, born under the law, to redeem those who were under the law, so that we might receive adoption as sons (Galatians 4:4).

When Jesus Christ walked the earth, He did so perfectly. In so doing, He was qualified to become the perfect sacrifice needed to atone for the sins of God's people. Christ became that sacrifice when He was crucified on the cross.

Christ did not deserve suffering and death. But it happened according to the Father's plan to make Him the One who justifies those who trust in His name. This plan was secured by His resurrection from the dead. And all who believe in Him live as His adopted children, and part of a new humanity.

It is from this new humanity the Dominion Mandate finds its restoration. Those who belong to Christ no longer live for themselves, but for the One who redeemed them. And they show forth their faithfulness by seeking to obey His Great Commission to disciple the nations (Matthew 28:18-20).

Today, Jesus reigns at the right hand of the Father, waiting until all His enemies be made a footstool for His feet (Hebrews 10:12-13). In time, the renewed Dominion Mandate will be consummated in the new heavens and the new earth (2 Peter 3:13).

Aspects of Redemption
The redemption God is working out in the world has

several aspects to it. Keep these aspects in mind, because they'll help give you the perspective you need to remain faithful to Him.

First, there is a definite aspect. What Christ accomplished through his death, resurrection, and ascension guarantees the Father's plan of redemption will come to completion—and the Dominion Mandate will be fulfilled. It will not fail. Christ's death fully paid for the sins of His people. By His resurrection, Christ triumphed over death and brought new life to the world. And in His ascension to the right hand of the Father we have assurance that Christ rules today, and the whole world will be subject to Him.

> What Christ accomplished through His death, resurrection, and ascension guarantees the Father's plan of redemption will come to completion—and the Dominion Mandate will be fulfilled. It will not fail.

Second, there's a progressive aspect. God's redemption of the world is not instantaneous. It happens over time. As His people multiply and grow in maturity, the world is conquered as their light expels the darkness. As this transformation occurs, both individuals and institutions are changed. And the whole world is moved toward a more glorious future.

Third, there is a final aspect of redemption at the consummation of history. When this happens, Satan will be destroyed. His influence on the world will be permanently removed as the Lord renders His final judgment. The transformation of the world will be complete. Every knee will bow and every tongue will confess that Jesus Christ is Lord (Philippians 2:9-11).

God has restored His original purpose for mankind. That purpose is being fulfilled through the redemption secured by Jesus. The Dominion Mandate that was hindered by sin is now able to be pursued with hope. And the corruption that mars the world will one day be completely overcome by grace.

Dominion through History

Is history just a random collection of events? Do people, rulers, and nations come and go without reason? That's how many see it. But with Christ's reign, history is headed toward a particular destination. It's the story of God's grace being worked out in space and time to complete the Dominion Mandate.

As we've seen, this mandate was first given at the beginning of creation. Even right after the Fall the mandate remained in force. We know this because after God judged the world with the great flood, He reissued the orders to fill the earth and subdue it (Genesis 9:1, 7).

Along with this reaffirmation, came the institution of human government, which was needed to bring order and justice to a sinful world. Also, in this situation came the need for those who would carry out the Dominion Mandate by bringing remedies to a fallen world through a variety of new callings, such as law and medicine.

By design, God has always intended to use His chosen people to lead the way in fulfilling the Dominion Mandate. As His people follow His Word, they serve as an example to the nations, to direct them to the Lord. God's people are to function as the salt of the earth and the light of the world. They are a city on a hill (Matthew 5:13-16).

Even now God is actively extending His kingdom through history, displacing the city of man with the city of God. This comes not by oppressive means, but as His people serve others in the power of the Spirit. When His people are faithful as servants, they increasingly find themselves in positions of authority and increased wealth, which brings even more opportunities to serve.

> The kingdom advances not by oppressive means, but through service in the power of the Spirit.

The growth of the kingdom is slow. The Bible describes it as beginning like a small seed, and enlarging as if under the influence of leaven (Matthew 13:31-33). When it comes to the kingdom's progress, we need to be patient. History has its setbacks. Yet though these setbacks come, they should not shake our confidence. God has initiated the renewal of His creation, and it won't be stopped. It will be brought to its glorious completion.

A New Humanity

The reason God works through His people to fulfill the Dominion Mandate is that they represent a new humanity. Each member of this new humanity is a new creature in Christ, who has experienced a renewal of the image of God. Thanks to this renewal, God's people serve as a new beginning for the work of transformation God has in mind for the whole world.

This transformation from a life of darkness to light is part of God's work of grace in the lives of His people. With this comes a whole new purpose, along with specially ordained works to be carried out in the world.

Through these works, God's people build others up and extend Christ's kingdom according to their gifts and opportunities. These gifts and opportunities vary according to the wisdom of He who distributes them, so there's no reason for anyone to begrudge his appointed area of service. What matters is to serve well in the place you find yourself.

Don't overlook the extent of your influence on other people. Your life makes more of a mark on others than you think. So be mindful that even the simplest actions can help or hinder the fulfillment of the Dominion Mandate because of their impact on others.

We need to remember that our actions influence those who live beyond our lifetime as well. On the negative side, the Bible says that God visits the iniquity of the fathers on the third and fourth generations of those who hate Him. On the positive side, He shows mercy to thousands of them that love Him and keep His commandments (Exodus 20:5, 6).

What you do with your life matters. It sends ripples into the lives of others far beyond what you can comprehend. And, though you may not be able to see the effects of your actions now, they will all be remembered on the last day by the One who judges rightly.

It's been over twenty years since I had the opportunity to meet with the late Dr. Paul Lindstrom, a pioneer in the Christian school movement. Although we chatted for only about fifteen minutes, our time together had an irreversible impact on me. And it had nothing to do with what Dr. Lindstrom said. It had to do with what he gave me.

43

Upon saying good-bye, Dr. Lindstrom graciously gave me a couple of volumes from the then recently published Biblical Blueprint Series. To be honest, the books sat on my shelf for at least a couple of years. But when I finally read them, they changed my life.

Up until that time, I believed the basic Christian message was about personal piety and how to get to heaven. But upon reading these books, I learned the message is far more comprehensive. I learned the Christian life is about more than working on my character while waiting for God to deliver us. It's about applying the Bible's principles to every aspect of life, and doing so in order to advance the kingdom of God.

Living as a New Creature

To live as a new creature in Christ brings hope that nothing else can. Because this is the only way you're able to live as you were designed to.

But what does living as a new creature in Christ mean practically?

First, it means your life is in Christ. To the extent you live in union with Christ, you will experience the fullness of life God has for you. It's in Christ you find your value. And it's through Him you bring value to the lives of others. Through Christ alone you are able to serve as a co-creator with God and bring His dominion to the world.

Also, living as a new creature means you function as a "dominion man" (or woman) by ruling well over your domain. By rule, more is meant than just keeping things under control. It means developing what's under your care. Cultivating what needs to be cultivated. Saving and restoring where necessary. Applying wisdom to bring about the best outcomes, and always aiming for the glory of God. In a word, to live as a dominion man is to be about "transformation," which is only made possible by the grace of God.

Finally, to live as a new creature is to live by faith. God's original plan for Adam was that he would extend His rule and develop the world as he trusted God and His Word. But Adam did not trust, and all who have been born after him are resistant to trust Him, too. Yet with Christ's redemption has come the ability to live out God's design. By grace we are able to live by faith in Him. As we do, we carry on the Dominion Mandate and experience the purpose God has for us.

The most important practical point about redemption is that it's not something to merely understand theologically. It's to be lived. Because it's as we live out our redemption, the world benefits. Not only that, we benefit. As we put into practice what the Spirit works in our hearts, we become like the One who has redeemed our lives.

The Hope of Victory

Christians agree there will be victory at the end of the age. Christ will come; there will be judgment, a separation of the sheep from the goats, and a casting out of God's enemies. Christ's rivals will be no more, and there will be a consummation of the new creation.

But what about before that time? Is there hope of observable improvement in our world *in this age*? Can we expect the advance of God's kingdom in the world will

45

make a tangible difference on this side of eternity? Will there be victory in time as well as eternity?

There are plenty who would answer "no" to these questions. And so we have this belief that all we can do is seek to hold ground the best we can and wait for Christ's return.

> Can we expect the advance of God's kingdom in the world to make a tangible difference on this side of eternity?

But should the prospects for the Dominion Mandate be so pessimistic? Let's consider this a little further.

When God first gave the Dominion Mandate, He did so intending it would be fulfilled. And because He is sovereign, nothing can stop God's plans from coming to completion. Even after sin entered the world, His intent continued. This is why he reissued the mandate and provided redemption for the human race.

Through history we see instances of success and failure regarding the mandate. When God's people, Israel, were faithful, they had health, peace, abundance, and influence on the surrounding nations. The reign of Solomon illustrates this best as the mandate was clearly being fulfilled in Israel's glory days. But when God's people disobeyed, they were cursed, and it was a step back for the Dominion Mandate.

In a similar way, the advance of Western Civilization and the founding of America should also be seen as progress for the Dominion Mandate—to the extent they've incorporated biblical principles. Though it's politically incorrect to say it, we can give credit to the Dominion Mandate and biblical standards for the blessings we've enjoyed in the West. And it's as these principles have been forsaken, both America and Western Civilization have been in decline.

This is all in keeping with what the Bible teaches. The Bible promises there will be positive and negative sanctions in history for obedience and disobedience (Leviticus 26, Deuteronomy 28). It does so as a way to encourage behaviors and activities that will lead to the mandate's fulfillment.

We shouldn't ignore the places the Bible speaks optimistically about the future. When it tells of a time coming before the end of the age when there will be remarkable fruitfulness and longevity, this should give us great hope (Isaiah 65). Hope that the gospel will influence the nations for good before the end of all things. And when the Bible speaks of the knowledge of the Lord filling the earth as the waters cover the sea, this should give us energy to persevere (Habakkuk 2:14).

Recall also, Jesus directed us to pray that His kingdom would come on earth as it is in heaven (Matthew 6:10). And, He commissioned us to make disciples—not merely converts—of all nations (Matthew 28:18-20). Surely, Jesus gave these instructions with the expectation of success, not failure. And this vision of success should infuse your own response to the Dominion Mandate.

The Bible presents Jesus Christ as already reigning, with His kingdom on the advance over time. The day is coming when after a brief, final period of rebellion, every resistant power and authority will be subdued. When this happens, Jesus will present a renewed world and redeemed humanity to His Father (1 Corinthians 15:24).

The fulfillment of this is a process. And God directs you to be an active part of the process as you live faithfully according to His call upon your life.

The process of fulfilling God's purpose may be slow, but it's sure. There is hope for the future. "For the kingdom is the Lord's, and He rules over the nations" (Psalm 22:28).

Sin and death delivered a serious blow to the Dominion Mandate—but it has been resurrected in Jesus. As we are faithful to obey Christ's Great Commission to disciple the nations and observe all that He commanded, we pursue the Dominion Mandate today.

There is no question the Dominion Mandate will be fulfilled. The only question is how you will respond and be a part of it.

Central to the Dominion Mandate is the truth that Jesus Christ is Lord. Because He is Lord, we are to worship and serve Him with our lives.

As we present ourselves to Him in worship, He renews us by His grace and makes us part of a new humanity.

As we, in the power of the Spirit, live as part of this renewed humanity, we fulfill our purpose and carry out the Dominion Mandate with the work He gives us.

Because Jesus is Lord, we are assured that our effort— no matter how small—contributes to the fulfillment of His plan for the world.

> "And He who sits on the throne said,
> 'Behold, I am making all things new.'"
> ~ Revelation 21:5

Summary

◆ For the Dominion Mandate to provide a sustainable purpose for living there needs to be reason to believe it can be accomplished.

◆ God has instituted a plan of redemption so the Dominion Mandate remains in force and will one day be brought to completion.

◆ God's plan of redemption has three aspects: definite, progressive, and final.

◆ History is the story of God's grace being worked out in space and time to fulfill the Dominion Mandate.

◆ Those who have faith in Christ are part of a new humanity. It is through this new humanity that God brings transformation to the world.

◆ Those who are part of the new humanity are new creatures in Christ, who have been restored to live out God's design.

◆ The instructions of Jesus, as found in the Lord's Prayer and the Great Commission, anticipate the success of the Dominion Mandate.

◆ The day is coming when God's plan of redemption
will be complete, and the Dominion Mandate will be
fully accomplished.

Make it Personal

1. Why is God's plan of redemption the hope of
humanity?

2. Membership in the new humanity comes through
faith in Jesus Christ. Is your faith in Christ?

3. How does God's plan of redemption affect your view
of the Dominion Mandate and the future?

PART TWO

APPLICATIONS

Chapter 4

Remember That You're Under Assignment

Your Life Belongs to God

". . . whether we live or die, we are the Lord's."
~ Romans 14:8

With Christ's work of redemption it's now possible for you to purposefully follow the Dominion Mandate. But just because it's possible doesn't mean you will. Our fallen nature does not give up easily. It keeps pushing the idea that you are the hub of all that takes place, and pursuing your own interests is what really matters.

But God designed the world to function entirely different. He made it so we would be God-centered, not self-centered. If you ignore this, you'll suffer harm. **But if you align yourself with God and His created order, you'll be in a position to fulfill your purpose and experience His favor.**

Autonomy

To be in a position to live out your purpose you need to resist autonomy. The word autonomy literally means "self-law," and it describes well the man who views the whole universe as revolving around him and his agenda.

He functions as a law unto himself, and his whole life is about working the world's system to his advantage.

The way of autonomy is standard fare in today's world. Whenever you hear encouragement to do it your own way or look out for number one, you can be almost positive the spirit of autonomy is at work.

This spirit is hard to escape. Not only does it flow from our fallen nature, it's reinforced by the world around us. The messages that surround you assume that you treat yourself as though you were the center on the solar system. And they reinforce a self-centered life.

Resisting the spirit of autonomy requires ongoing, conscious effort. You must resist this spirit if you are going to live out the purpose God has for you. The way to resist the spirit of autonomy is to live in submission to the Lord. It's to live as one under orders.

The autonomous man is always trying to create his own purpose and significance. This never ends because he lacks an anchor for his soul. Without an anchor, the issue of his purpose never finds closure. He might be busy with an impressive agenda, and even have some earthly accomplishments, but none of it is rooted in what lasts.

The autonomous life fits right in with the evolutionary worldview that's so much a part of the air we breathe. From a humanistic, evolutionary standpoint, the Dominion Mandate can only be about furthering one's own mission—not God's eternal purpose. But those who follow their own personal, autonomous mission operate outside of God's design, and miss the purpose He has for their lives.

Serve the Sovereign Creator

The alternative to living autonomously is to yield your life to God as the sovereign ruler over all. And live out the divine assignment He has for you.

God has made the world and is in charge of it. He has set it up for His own eternal purpose, and He's designed how it's to function. To accept this is the beginning of contentment and rest. It's the starting point for anyone who wants to find his purpose in the world.

To live by faith in God as the Lord over all brings simplicity to life. It brings relief from the ongoing quest to find yourself and your place in the world. You don't have to keep figuring out why you're here. You're free, instead, to focus on your own role in following the Dominion Mandate.

> To accept that God made the world and is in charge of it is the starting point for anyone who wants to find his purpose in the world.

Living in submission to the Lord also removes confusion about how you're to live your life. That's because He's given us a standard to live by. And that standard is found in His Word.

Be prepared for those who say that living your life for the Lord is a way to escape your responsibilities in the real world. Actually, it's the opposite. When you acknowledge the Lord as the ruler of your life, you also accept He's given you orders as to what you're to be doing in the real world. And we show ourselves most responsible when we follow those orders.

Inescapable Sovereignty

If you find it difficult to submit to God's rule over you, this may help: realize that the concept of sovereignty is inescapable, and then follow that thought to its conclusion. You, as an individual, are sovereign, a group of rulers is sovereign, or God is sovereign. These are the options.

The first two options are easy to dismiss.

Think of any personal problem you would like to make go away. The fact you can't make it go away by your own power shows you aren't sovereign. If you were, you would have made the problem disappear long ago. But since you can't, it reveals that you, as an individual, are not sovereign.

Now, let's take a pressing problem the world faces today, like the debt crisis. This problem has hung over nations for years. If the rulers of the world were sovereign, they could have fixed this long ago. But they're not sovereign. Their power is limited. They have to deal with the reality of God's principles as they work themselves out in the world.

That leaves the third option; God is the ruler over all. The Bible tells us the Lord has established His throne in the heavens and His sovereignty rules over all (Psalm 103:19). Our fallen nature may resist this, but it's the truth. God rules over everything—even hardship and disasters, which He ultimately uses for the good of those who love Him and are called according to His purpose (Romans 8:28). We can be sure of this because He planned and brought about the death and resurrection of Jesus Christ from the dead, for our benefit.

NOTE: Someone might object that I've missed an option, and claim that nature is sovereign. But this doesn't work.

Sovereignty implies personality. For there to be a rule, there needs to be a ruler. Even though we speak a lot of Mother Nature, there's no such lady.

Fairness and Freedom

One common reason why you might have difficulty forsaking your autonomy and turning to the Lord as the ruler of your life is this: it seems to violate your natural ideas about fairness and freedom.

The questions go like this. What's wrong with living as an autonomous human being? Isn't it unfair of God to expect us to live any other way? And doesn't living in submission to Him take away our freedom?

These are legitimate questions. Let's consider them.

The place to begin is by looking at God, and then ourselves.

Who is God, anyway? Well, He is the Creator of all things. He is the one who made you and me. He knows all things, and is all-powerful. He owns everything. He has designed the world, and has done so for a purpose. He also provides redemption through His Son so that His purpose will be accomplished.

Who are we? We are creatures made in God's image. We are unable to sustain ourselves. We are totally dependent on God and His grace to not only remain alive but do anything in this world. Everything we have has been given to us. Without Him we have nothing and are nothing.

When you look at the contrast between God and us, questions about God's fairness melt away. He is the maker. What can we say? Is it not fair for the maker to do what He will with what He's made? What complaint can the clay bring against the potter?

O.K., but what about freedom? Does not living in submission to God take away our freedom and all it means to be fully human?

To answer this question the notion of freedom held by most needs to be challenged.

It's commonly assumed to be free you must be able to do anything you desire. But there is no absolute freedom in this sense. You know this already because you are aware there are certain things you can't do, no matter how much you want to. You are not free to fly, or live under water. You can't eat an endless supply of pizza, or drink unlimited glasses of beer. You weren't designed to.

And this gets to the heart of what true freedom is all about.

Freedom is not found in doing whatever you can imagine or obeying whatever impulse you feel. Actually, obeying every impulse can be a form of slavery. To be free is to live fully in keeping with your design. And do so in a way that brings joy and satisfaction. And this God provides to all who turn to Him. When we submit to Him, we know the truth—not just intellectually, but by way of experience—and this truth sets us free.

> Freedom is not found in doing whatever you can imagine or following whatever impulse you feel.

Submission to the Lord is the only way to find genuine freedom. And there's no changing it.

He is the Creator and we are His creatures. But there's no reason to be frustrated by this. By living in submission to the Lord, you'll be much freer than you ever could be by following whatever natural desires may rise in your heart.

Plus, it's only in serving Him that you'll be in a position to receive the purpose He has for you—and freely live it out.

You Have an Assignment

God has assigned humanity to fill the earth and bring His rule to the world. It's in this way we glorify Him, and also find our joy. God places this call on every human being.

But we must do more than see this assignment in the abstract. Because it will only be fulfilled as individuals like you and me make this assignment personal.

To take this assignment on yourself, see yourself as a steward who has been entrusted with an important task. This is fitting, because a steward is exactly what you are. God has given you a post to fill. And He has given you the gifts and resources and opportunities He has so you would further the assignment you have.

This again is all part of God's order. There is a harmony of interests shared by humanity that furthers the interests of all. And there is a division of labor whereby each one has his place to serve for the greater good of all.

The place you have in this system is significant.

No one can do what you do. Of course, God could have put someone else in your spot. But when God gives you certain gifts to use in a certain time and place, you are the one to do it, and there's really no one else.

With the assignments God gives us comes accountability.

There's accountability that comes through others that God puts in our lives. And there's accountability that comes from knowing God will evaluate our work on the last day. At that time, He will judge how we've done with the talents He's given us. As you know this day is coming, strive to live in such a way to hear Him say, "Well done good and faithful servant" (Matthew 25:14-30).

A while back there was a story circulating online about the regrets of the dying. The regrets were documented by a palliative care nurse who spent time tending to the dying in the last weeks of their lives.

What was the most common regret shared by those who knew they were in their final days?

"I wish I'd had the courage to live a life true to myself, not the life others expected of me."

As a pastor who has conversed with people on their deathbeds, I can confirm this is common. And it's a good reminder why it's important to discover what God has for you to do in this life now—and do it.

There's No Neutrality
We as human beings like to play in neutral territory. It seems safer to us that way.

But there is no neutrality with God.

When it comes to relating to God there is no middle

ground. There is no "I sort of want it His way and I sort of don't." As Jesus put it, you are either for Him or against Him (Matthew 12:30). No fence-sitting allowed.

Realizing there's no neutrality is important to you for two reasons.

First, it helps you determine where you stand. You cannot serve God and mammon. You have to decide—are you going to live the way He calls you to or not? Do you want His best purpose for your life, or your own purpose?

Second, remembering there's no neutrality helps to keep you on track. When making decisions about your direction, knowing that nothing is neutral helps prevent you from trying to hide in some mushy middle ground. When there's no neutrality, the choice becomes clear. Are you going to pursue the Dominion Mandate as it relates to your life, or are you not?

In generations before us there was a word commonly used that sums up the theme of this chapter. That word is "duty." In our day duty has become a dirty word. It sounds oppressive and confining to contemporary ears.

But in the light of the mandate God has for us, there's nothing undesirable about doing your duty.

Duty is the fitting response to the One who created us and gives us His grace. And it's as you do your duty out of gratitude that you discover the purpose and meaning you're looking for.

One of the obvious ways to help discover your purpose is to consider your duties. Take time to think through what your duties at present actually are. As you do, it will help you find the assignment God has for you at this point in your life.

61

Always remember, you're under orders. God has an assignment for you, and by grace you are to do your best to complete it, as you respond to the love He has shown you.

Your life is to be God-centered, not self-centered.

Summary

◆ God is at the center of all He has made. We are able to fulfill our purpose when we align ourselves with His created order.

◆ By nature, we desire the path of autonomy, and live with ourselves at the center of it all. But to discover God's purpose for us, we must resist this tendency and live with Him at the center.

◆ We acknowledge God as the sovereign Lord as we submit to His Word.

◆ Freedom is found not in following our own desires, but in being able to live as God designed us to live.

◆ We've all been assigned to bring Christ's rule over His creation. We take on God's assignment for us when we serve Him with the gifts He has given us in the places He has us.

◆ There is a division of labor across humanity that contributes to the fulfillment of the Dominion Mandate.

◆ There is no neutrality when it comes to our relationship with the Lord. We are either consciously serving Him or we are not.

◆ Pursuing the Dominion Mandate is our duty as creatures made in God's image.

Make it Personal

1. How do you see the drive to autonomy being worked out in your life?

2. Where has the idea that freedom is living according to your own desires taken you?

3. What steps do you need to take now to fulfill the assignment God seems to have ordained for you?

Chapter 5

Practice Real World Spirituality

True Spirituality Seeks to Engage the World, Not Escape It

"For everything created by God is good, and nothing is to be rejected, if it is received with gratitude."
~ 1Timothy 4:4

When you hear of someone referred to as a very spiritual person, what kind of image comes to mind? Is it of a ghostly figure clutching a Bible? Is it of a person who seems inhuman, with little interest in the concerns of the world?

> What does it mean to be a spiritual person?

If that's the kind of picture that comes to mind, it's easy to understand why. The idea of a spiritual person as one who disconnects from normal life is a common one. It's an image that scares a lot of people from taking a closer look at their own spirituality.

This ethereal perception of what it means to be a spiritual person is misleading. It falsely represents what it means to be spiritual and because it's widely held, it's extremely destructive.

This view of spirituality doesn't lead anyone to live out his purpose and have a positive impact on the world, but true spirituality will. That is why possessing it is essential.

So let's distinguish between true spirituality and false spirituality.

False Spirituality

Going all the way back to the philosopher Plato there existed a worldview known as dualism. One of the tenets of dualism is the immaterial, spiritual world is superior to the physical world. Because dualists see the physical world as inferior, they believe the ideal is to escape it.

Dualism's influence has led many to think a truly spiritual person is someone who does not concern himself with matters of this world. In fact, it's often assumed the less someone involves himself with this world, the more spiritual he must be.

The idea that the physical world is inferior brings destructive results. It keeps people from living out their purpose, and it prevents them from engaging the world in a way that would improve the lives of others.

Have you known people who refuse to get involved and help others in a tangible way because it seems unspiritual or beneath them? Have you come across those who are so absorbed in the life to come they contribute little to life in the here and now? Do you know people who won't stand up for what's right because their view of spirituality has led them to become too passive and nice?

If so, you know folks infected with dualism.

You want to be able to recognize dualism when you see it. It's a false view of God's world that's connected to a false view of spirituality. It promotes a kind of ethereal spirituality that holds you back from living out the purpose God has for you in the real world.

One common expression of dualism is Gnosticism. According to Gnostics, our real need is to discover the divinity within ourselves. And the way to salvation is to possess some secret knowledge known only to those enlightened. As a consequence, Gnostics are inclined to dismiss the created world. And they justify their disengagement by claiming what really matters is having the right thinking.

There are also Gnostics who use their elevated view of knowledge to justify immoral behavior. According to them, how they handle their bodies or live in the world is not a concern, because they supposedly have hidden insight the rest of us lack.

It doesn't take much to realize how damaging this way of thinking can be. Yet this worldview is more widespread than you might think. There are many who find it attractive because it is agreeable with their pride or desire for pleasure.

Biblical Spirituality

In contrast to the creation-denying errors of dualism and Gnosticism, the Bible presents God as the Creator of the physical world. Because He made it, God does not view the physical world as inferior. In fact, when God saw everything that He made He pronounced it "very good" (Genesis 1:31). The Bible also tells us that we are to partake of the blessings of the created world, and receive them with thanks (1 Timothy 4:4).

It's by understanding God created the physical world for our good that we are able to come to an accurate view of spirituality, that doesn't deny God's creation, but properly engages it.

So what is a true, biblical understanding of spirituality?

To live as a spiritual person is to recognize that God made you in His image, and has commissioned you to live your life for His glory. This is accomplished by following His mandate to fill the earth and subdue it as you walk according to His Spirit. As a spiritual person, you are to live in constant dependence on God's grace so you can actively carry out what He has given you to do.

> True spirituality does not retreat from the world.

True spirituality does not retreat from the world. It pursues God's call to dominion at every opportunity. When people practice true spirituality, it's comprehensive and world-changing. It's not compartmentalized to some private area of life, but seeks to apply God's Word from the doctor's office to the marketplace and from the school room to the courthouse.

True spirituality as described here is not practiced in one's own power and understanding. It's practiced through God's wisdom and strength.

The basis for viewing spirituality in this ambitious, engaging way is that Jesus Christ is Lord. Jesus came to redeem the planet. And through the Holy Spirit, He is bringing renewal to the whole world. God has called us to be a part of this renewal as we bring His grace and truth to bear in every area of life.

God Has Set the Pattern

No one would accuse God of being unspiritual for occupying Himself with the physical world. So it makes sense to pay attention to the way He developed the world. When we do, it sets up a pattern for us to follow.

When God first created, He didn't do it all at once. He did it over a period of days, and it involved certain steps. After making the waters below, for example, He separated them and dry land appeared (Genesis 1:9, 10).

Notice the pattern here. God took hold of what He made, broke it down, and then restructured it.

This is the same pattern we are to follow as we pursue the Dominion Mandate. **We're to take what God has provided us, work with it, and reconfigure it into something better and more valuable than it was before.** This is what happens whenever a house is constructed. The builder takes wood, cuts it into pieces, and puts it back together in a more developed form for someone to live in.

There's another pattern God set that's worth our attention. It's found in the Garden of Eden. The Garden was a type of sanctuary. This garden was set up as a starting point. From this point, God's intent was to develop the whole world as mankind moves from The Garden outward.

Again, observe the pattern. God starts in a sanctuary—a place of peace and rest—and works out from there. So, as the first man went from a place of rest, where he was strengthened for his dominion efforts, we're to do the same.

This is why the Scripture directs us to begin our week in a place of rest in God's sanctuary. As Adam's first full day was one of worship, so should the first day of our week. God made us to worship, and it's in His presence that He receives us, instructs us, feeds us, and sends us out with a blessing to go and advance His kingdom in the world.

As we follow this pattern ourselves, we share the work of our Creator in bringing value to the world. And with His Spirit working in us, we use the gifts He has given to contribute to the new creation.

Bringing Value to the World

It's noteworthy that in the marketplace it's the creation of value that's rewarded. And here we can discern a connection between our everyday labors and the purpose God has for us. As you strive to bring real value to others in the place God has put you, you're playing a part in extending His mandate.

Let me give you an example. As I write this book, I'm sitting in a comfortable desk chair. When you consider all it took to make this chair and get it into my office, it is not unreasonable to say there were probably hundreds of people involved in the process. That's no exaggeration. Once you include designers, producers of raw materials, manufacturers, truck drivers, retailers, and so on.

For each part of the process, the role played by those involved may have seemed insignificant. But each part was necessary to bring the finished product to completion and get it to me for my benefit. Because I have the chair, I'm able to be more productive in my work. And I'm able to make a greater contribution to further the Dominion Mandate myself.

The same principle is active in what God has given you to

do. You may not see your task as all that important, but you should, because it's part of a larger effort to follow the Dominion Mandate. And it's as you do what He's given you to do faithfully that you will find your joy and satisfaction.

Today's New Spirituality in Business

The fact that God has made us spiritual beings can't be escaped. One of the ways you can see this is through the recent attention given to spirituality in the business world.

Both online and offline businesses are paying more attention to human factors, especially human spirituality. The increased emphasis on empathy, connecting with others, transparency, being yourself and authenticity is now common, and viewed as a key part of doing business today.

Hardline, old-school business people may consider this to be nothing but new-age fluff, but this trend actually reveals something substantial. It reveals even in the world of work you can't get away from the reality that God has created human beings with certain spiritual aspirations.

> Even in the world of work you can't escape the reality that God has created human beings with certain spiritual aspirations.

The new interest we see in spirituality in the business world presents an opportunity. But to really capitalize on the value of this trend, we need to see it as more than a vague interest in generic spirituality. It needs to be identified as an expression of the God-given desire to find one's place in the world He made and it must be channeled to serve the Dominion

71

Mandate.

God designed us all with a desire to have our work and efforts be meaningful. And it's the practice of genuine spirituality that allows us to experience this in our daily activities. Realizing this as you assess your own gifts and opportunities is an essential step toward finding your place in the world.

Understanding the Spiritual Options That Face Us

It's often assumed any indicator of spiritual interest is a good sign. It might be, but it isn't necessarily so, because not all expressions of spirituality are the same.

In general, three forms of spirituality are circulating today.

First, is escapism, which has a version for both those who are Christians and those who are not.

The Christian escapist retreats from this world while he waits for the eternal world to come. In the meantime, he may try to get all the enjoyment out of the world he can. But his focus is on life on the other side. And he hopes that Jesus will take him home before any serious suffering starts.

The non-Christian escapist gives little thought to matters of eternal significance. Instead he's out to maximize his pleasure in the here and now, and hope for the best. He may be optimistic or pessimistic, but in either case he doesn't seem to pay much attention to the big ideas at play in the world around him.

The second form of spiritual expression out there today is what's been called humanistic power religion. Here faith is in mankind, and its ability to control and shape the world without any divine assistance. This is the type of spirituality that dominates in our media, schools and government institutions.

Over time, this spirituality leads to a system that is centralized around an elite ruling class. In other words, it leads to tyranny. As this group gains more power, its corruption and inability to rule for the good of the people becomes more evident. When this happens, the people become restless and open to breaking free from the status quo. There are signs that this is beginning to happen today.

The third form of spirituality available is dominion religion. With this expression of spirituality there is a desire to develop the world for the benefit of others and the glory of God. This development occurs as God's people are serious about applying His Word to every area of life. It also involves a willingness to make sacrifices to further His kingdom.

Although Christians have held this view during much of history, only a minority of Christians seem to be aware of it today. Most Christians, at least in America, are of the escapist variety. They see the value of their faith as it applies to their own personal piety, but don't seem to expect it to have much influence in the world.

The kind of change our world needs will only come about with a change in worldview where men do not seek power over one another, but seek the power of God to build His kingdom together. There's only one spiritual option out there today that can bring this about, and it's the practice of dominion spirituality.

Dominion Spirituality
The Dominion Mandate cannot be fulfilled when people

seek to escape the challenges of this world or place their hope in humanistic power. It's only when there's an eagerness to practice a spirituality geared toward dominion that the world will progressively come under Christ's rule and be blessed with His favor.

So what do those who practice dominion spirituality look like? Their lives are marked in the following ways.

First, they know who they are. They live with awareness that they belong to the Lord, and that He loves them and has called them to do a work in this world. They have a secure identity found not in their own achievements, but by living in union with Jesus Christ.

Second, they realize their ongoing need for grace. They act on this need for grace by drawing near to the Lord through the means He provides us. These include worship, Bible study, prayer, service, fellowship with others, and so on. Through the faithful use of these means, God supplies in abundance the strength and direction needed to live a life of dominion.

Third, they are devoted to applying God's Word to all of life. They see every area of existence as coming under the Bible's authority and wisdom, and seek to apply the principles of Scripture to their labors. Those who practice dominion spirituality have the expectation that as they apply God's Word faithfully, it will not only transform them, but transform the world as well.

Finally, they seek to please and honor the Father in all they do. And they are filled with peace, hope, and joy as they know He rules over all, and that their labor is not in vain.

To know your purpose and fulfill it, you need to understand what it is to live out your spirituality. Stay far from spiritualities that deny your need to engage the world, or those that seek to manipulate it through your own power. Instead, nurture the spirituality which seeks to further your renewal in Jesus Christ and develop God's creation by submitting to Him and serving with His gifts.

Franklin Sanders publishes a successful newsletter each month called *The Moneychanger*. In it he provides a no nonsense analysis of financial news and cultural trends. I always enjoy reading his publication when it arrives because it *demonstrates* what it is to live out your principles in the real world.

In one issue Sanders addressed the problem of losing heart, a relevant theme for sure. Doubt and depression come easily in a degenerate age like ours. And, the slow, uneven advance of God's kingdom can make it appear He's abandoned the field altogether. But there's never any reason to question Christ's total victory. Little by little the whole earth, including every man, will bow to His rule.

With this confidence we're to keep toiling away at our own workbenches. But be careful where you fix your attention. If all you do is look at the sawdust around your feet, your efforts will seem futile. But if you labor with an eye to eternity, you can be assured your toil is not in vain, as it's a part of a much larger work of God.

It's this kind of perspective that demonstrates true spirituality.

Summary

◆ There is a false spirituality prevalent that believes the immaterial world is superior to the physical world. For those who believe this, the ideal of any person is to escape the physical world.

◆ The idea that the physical world is inferior is destructive, as it serves to keep people from engaging the world in a constructive way.

◆ The Bible teaches the created world is good. So it follows that true spirituality engages the world and seeks dominion over it, as God has commanded us.

◆ When God created the world, He set a pattern for us to follow when He took hold of the world and restructured it. We, too, are to take hold of the world and develop it in this way.

◆ The recent attention to spirituality in the business world reflects mankind's built-in spiritual aspirations. These aspirations need to be brought to serve the Dominion Mandate.

◆ The three main competing spiritualities today are escapism, humanistic power religion, and dominion religion.

◆ Those who practice dominion spirituality know they belong to God, continually seek His grace, and devote themselves to applying the Bible to all of life.

Make it Personal

1. How has your view of spirituality affected the way you've lived?

2. In what ways can you see your work reflecting dominion spirituality?

3. What prevents you from practicing dominion spirituality?

Chapter 6

Don't Be Afraid of Work, Embrace It

To Accomplish Your Purpose You Have to Take Responsibility for the Work God Has for You

*"Whatever your hand finds to do,
do it with all your might."*
~ Ecclesiastes 9:10

You've probably heard the advice. If you want to get ahead in your endeavors, look at what everyone else is doing—and do the opposite. That's a good thought to start this chapter.

There are plenty of people who want to find their purpose in life and live it out. They think about it every day, yet few are willing to take responsibility and do the work necessary for it to happen. Those who do reap rewards for their efforts.

Marketing expert Dan Kennedy has described how most people live their lives in a way that makes me laugh every time I think about. He said most people walk around with their umbilical cords in theirs hands looking for a place to plug in so they can enjoy the life they're looking for.

If only it were that easy.

Anything worthwhile requires hard work and willingness to take responsibility. This is certainly true when it comes to finding and fulfilling the purpose God has for you.

What Do You Think of Work?

Today's general attitude toward work isn't too positive. For most, work is a necessary evil. And Friday can't come soon enough.

True, there are many who love their work. They look forward to it every day. There are others who recognize the problem is not so much with the concept of work, but the particular work they have to do. They just don't like *that* work.

But still, the point stands. There's a widespread problem people have with work. And if we're going to find our purpose and place in fulfilling the Dominion Mandate, we must have a strong theology of work.

> God gave mankind work to participate with Him in the glorious project of developing the world.

Doing this is not hard. The Bible gives us what we need to understand.

From the beginning God gave us work to do. He had Adam laboring before the Fall, so work was not given as a form of punishment. God gave mankind work to participate with Him in the glorious project of developing the world.

With the Fall, God cursed the ground, and work became difficult. Every vocation has its thorns and thistles and

80

results come only from the sweat of our brow.

But the struggle our work involves is not without purpose. It prompts us to seek God's grace and mercy for success.

Though work is difficult, our labors are not fruitless. Along with the redemption brought by Christ, came the restoration of work to its meaningful purpose—the fulfillment of the Dominion Mandate. Your work is more than a means to put bread on the table. It's a way to partake in the building of the kingdom.

Today, trying to escape work as much as possible seems to be the norm. But when we see the connection between work and God's purpose, there's a new motivation for our efforts.

What About the 4-Hour Work Week?

Recently I had a conversation with one of my sons about the popular book called *The 4-Hour Work Week*. He was inspired by the title, and I was a little concerned he might adopt an unrealistic view of what it takes to succeed. So I initiated a conversation with him.

I began by mentioning that I'm certain the author works more than four hours a week. I've seen him in too many settings promoting his four hour work week idea.

My son replied by saying, "Yeah, but he doesn't have to work more than four hours a week. He's found a way to support himself in that amount of time, but he works more than he needs to because he's doing what he loves."

That's a good point. If you find work that fits you, you're going to do it, even if you don't have to.

I suppose it's possible to run a successful business from

an iPad at the beach. But just because someone is able to do it doesn't mean that's necessarily the way he'll spend his life. This is especially true if he understands the Dominion Mandate, because it will drive him to use his extra time for activities more important than working on a tan.

Hindrances to Work

If work is good, why do we seek to avoid it?

Part of the reason has to do with the thorns and thistles that came with the Fall. Work is demanding. So the desire to avoid it comes naturally. But there are also other hindrances that keep many people from doing the work God has for them.

Here are five typical obstacles that keep people like you and me from working as we should. Beware of them, because these are among the most common reasons people miss out on experiencing their God-given purpose.

Entitlement Mentality. This is the idea that somebody owes you, or that you've already paid your dues, so someone else should cover for you. When you're afflicted with the entitlement mentality, you've essentially decided you're O.K. with being a parasite instead of a producer. The entitlement mentality runs deep in our society. Watch out for it.

Feeling Like a Victim. It is closely related to the entitlement mentality, but with a twist. Those with this outlook believe they've been hurt in some way. It may be perceived or real. In either case, they're convinced they've been cheated. And because of it, they believe it's a matter of justice that they don't pay their way. Those who play the victim card find it easy to look to others to carry their load.

Laziness. Garden variety laziness. Not much to explain here. The lazy man would rather loaf than exert himself and achieve. He's bored with life and can't figure out why. The Dominion Mandate is just what he needs to rouse him from his slumber. It can happen if he's willing to consider the opportunities before him and exert a little energy, and follow through with some consistency.

Procrastination. This is the brother of laziness. The procrastinator believes he'll always have tomorrow. But He forgets that God has numbered his days. He watches the months go by and wonders why nothing changes. He remains today where he's always been. By wasting time he wastes his life. Don't let your life slip away because of procrastination.

Amusements. There's a place for recreation, and after expending much effort it may be just what you need to be re-created. A break can bring you back fresher. But amusements that often consume our breaks easily become excessive. At a minimum they become a distraction. In worse cases, they can become addictions or idols. Make sure you keep amusements in their place. Get dominion over them so they don't rule over you.

To establish good work habits and be as productive as possible you need to find a way to dodge your distractions. That way you can actually accomplish what you know you ought to get done.

One of the best ways I've found to control my distractions is to use a timer. I'll set the timer for 25 minutes and work hard to get as much done in that period as I can. Then, I'll take a five minute break. After four cycles, I'll then take a longer break. I can't tell you how many times I've said to myself, "No, you can't check that email until the timer goes off." This method requires discipline, but it works.

If you would like to learn more about this approach, search "The Pomodoro Technique." It has really helped me focus when I need to.

What's important is to find some way to actually work when you know you should be working.

Work and Responsibility

Overcoming the hindrances to work can be tough, but it can be done. And when you do overcome what hinders you, you'll find it rewarding.

So, what can we do to become better workers?

It starts with a simple observation. Work is called work for a reason—it's work!

There's the idea around today that work can be like play. And if you really like what you do, it's not work at all. I'm sorry, but this is just a ploy to get you to either buy into some unrealistic work opportunity or become discontent with your circumstances. Sure, people can enjoy their work so much they like it as much as their recreational activities. But work and play are not the same. Because work involves responsibility that play does not.

I have a brother who works for a professional sports team. A lot of people envy him for his position. To the outsider, it looks like his work would not be work at all, but play. The truth is, he puts in more hours and faces more pressure than most I know. You mean he can't just hang out with the players and come and go as he pleases? No. He has responsibilities. A lot of them.

Taking responsibility for the tasks God gives you is key to living out the purpose He has for your life. Without responsibility, there's little of significance that's accomplished.

Your current areas of responsibility serve as a proving ground. The better you do with the responsibilities before you now, the more you can be trusted with higher levels of authority and responsibility in the future. Pay attention to this principle. By adhering to it, you'll be on your way to reaching your maximum potential and bringing the greatest possible benefit to others.

When God first commissioned Adam, He charged Him to guard and cultivate The Garden. This was the responsibility God gave him, but Adam failed to do what he was supposed to do. To make matters worse, he didn't take responsibility for his failure.

Adam did not take responsibility for a simple reason. He was impatient and immature. He acted like a child. If he had patience and maturity he would have trusted God's Word and done what God instructed him to do.

There's a lot to be learned from Adam.

Think about it. When we don't take responsibility to do

what we should, what are we doing? We're acting like Adam. We're acting like children who don't want to do their work. But God wants us to be mature. He wants us equipped to partner with Him in making the world flourish.

Work is not just an earthly necessity. It's not just something we have to do to keep the lights on. It's a responsibility we have from God to play our part in His world. And when we embrace the work and responsibility He gives us, we experience life as mature adults.

> When we embrace the work and responsibility God gives us, we experience life as mature adults.

One reason we don't see the Dominion Mandate further advanced than we do is that there are too many who don't want to grow up. We are born not wanting to take responsibility or put forth effort. But as we grow and mature, we're to overcome this tendency. We're to take on work and responsibility gladly. Not just as a necessary evil.

God provided all that's necessary for the world to be developed. He also has a design for us to experience fulfillment. We experience both when we apply ourselves to the work He's given us to do.

Those who take responsibility and work hard at some honest endeavor are the most fulfilled people you will find. Choosing to join them is one of the wisest decisions you can make.

It's rarely recognized, but the contribution made by those in business toward fulfilling the Dominion Mandate has been enormous. Just think, for example, how much productivity can be attributed to Levi Strauss and his manufacture of blue jeans.

A more current illustration of an innovator who has made a remarkable contribution to the Dominion Mandate is a man named Gary Young.

After three years in a wheelchair because of a crippling logging accident, D. Gary Young began experimenting with essential oils to relieve his pain. Not only did the essential oils bring relief, they eventually worked to restore the feeling and mobility in his legs.

From this personal experience, Gary decided to share the healing properties of essential oils with the world. Gary's company, Young Living Essential Oils, has now become the world leader in therapeutic-grade essential oils. Its operation cultivates over 5,000 acres of land. The company's line of high quality natural products serves to improve the health of thousands of people daily.

Gary Young is self-conscious about his company's efforts to follow the Dominion Mandate. He not only talks about it at company meetings, but seeks to have it infuse the organization's vision as well. This focus has served the company well, and has helped to transform many lives— not just through the company's products, but through its many humanitarian efforts as well.

Changing the World

Ever since Adam the world has experienced development. This development has not occurred in a straight line. The reality of evil, along with human limitations, has led to many zigs and zags on the course of progress. But the general trajectory has been one of advancement.

People often romanticize the past. They speak of going back to the good old days. But the good old days had their problems, too. There were selfish and corrupt people back then, just as there are today. And, do you really want to go back to an era without indoor plumbing and running water?

The fact is history moves forward. There's no turning back. God is continually bringing changes and making all things new. Despite all the depravity and shortcomings of human beings, God is still working through people to fulfill the Dominion Mandate.

For some perspective on this, consider the following areas. There's been a lot of progress in each of them across the centuries.

- the preservation of life

- improvement in moral standards

- greater liberty and justice for all

- scientific advancement

- charity for the poor

- care for the sick and dying

- the elevation of women

- furthering of education

- improvement in labor and economic conditions

- increased standard of living

- development of literature, art and music

None of the developments in these areas happened spontaneously. Any positive change that's taken place has occurred because someone saw a need, and took initiative to address it. Those who took initiative subjected themselves to risks and hard work in doing so.

Consider some examples from history of those who brought about tremendous improvements to life through their efforts. Though we tend to take these achievements for granted today, those who accomplished them literally changed the world by playing their part in the Dominion Mandate.

- Emperor Justinian worked to make infanticide illegal.

- George Mueller ran orphanages to help thousands of children.

- Johann Gutenberg made possible the mass production of books.

- Christopher Columbus sailed uncharted waters to bring the gospel to new lands.

- William McGuffey created his "Readers" to teach young people how to read and live.

- William Bradford taught the importance of self-government as the basis of freedom.

- Francis Bacon developed the scientific method,

giving rise to modern science.

➢ Johannes Kepler discovered many laws of nature by "thinking God's thoughts after Him."

➢ John Calvin delivered teachings that led to the Protestant work ethic and abundant wealth creation.

➢ Basil of Caesarea founded the first hospital out of his concern for the sick.

➢ Florence Nightingale became the founder of modern nursing by answering a call to serve the suffering.

➢ Michelangelo used his genius to glorify God through art.

➢ William Shakespeare set a standard for literature that remains to this day.

➢ J.S. Bach devoted himself to music to elevate worship and bring glory to God alone.

➢ C.S. Lewis labored to become a master communicator and model writer.

This is just a sample of all who have exerted themselves and overcome obstacles to change our world for the better.

As we look at our world today, there is still much to be done. There are needs to be met and ideas to be implemented. This will only happen when people like you use your gifts and do something from the place God has you.

Don't wait for others to do what God may want you to venture out and do yourself.

What Motivates You?

People are motivated by different desires. Some are motivated by money, others by recognition, comfort, power, pleasure, and so on.

None of these motives deliver satisfaction. Even achieving long sought after goals doesn't bring the satisfaction we expect if it's these desires that are driving us.

There's a simple explanation for this.

God didn't make us to be motivated by self-centered aspirations. He designed us so we would be moved to serve Him. And do so by using the abilities He's given us to advance His work in the world. If that's not your motivation, your accomplishments will leave you empty.

When we're consistently motivated to serve God with our gifts, satisfaction comes easily. Not because achievement doesn't matter, but because we're able to trust God with the outcome of our efforts, having confidence He is using our efforts in ways unknown to us.

Surely, you've pursued some goals for a long time without results. Or, certain life changes have forced you to reset your goals, or take on an entirely new direction. When this happens, anxiety and frustration tend to surface as unexpected changes and delays can make it seem like our lives aren't going anywhere.

But there's no cause for grief here. As long as you are faithful doing what God calls you to do TODAY, you can be content. That's good news when you realize yesterday didn't go as you hoped, and tomorrow may not go as you expect.

God is at work through all your efforts. Disappointing

experiences will come, but they're not worth getting upset or angry over. God has a way of using even delays and setbacks to providentially direct our paths. And He is able to take us straight to His desired outcome through what seems like nothing but a maze to us.

Every day God has given you something to apply yourself to. It may be something big or small. But whatever your labor is, rejoice in it. This is God's gift to you. It's the work He has allotted to you in cooperation with His cause. And in this you can find contentment.

This doesn't mean you will necessarily like what you're doing at any given moment. It doesn't mean your work won't have issues that aggravate you. But it does mean if you're working as unto the Lord, you can be satisfied in it. You can be assured that what He has led you to do has its part in His larger plan for the world.

Have you ever wondered how someone who does menial labor like sweeping floors can be joyful, while someone with a prestigious, high-paying position can be full of gloom?

The answer may lie in the different ways they view work, and what drives them in their work. Because what motivates one in his work makes all the difference in whether he is satisfied or dissatisfied with what he is doing.

> Ever wonder how someone who does menial labor like sweeping floors can be joyful, while someone with a prestigious, high-paying position can be full of gloom?

What motivates you in your work? God has a purpose for

you in His mandate to fill and subdue the earth. When you discover what that purpose is, and take the responsibility to work at it, you'll find satisfaction in what you do.

All our work—even mowing the lawn—has its place in God's plan to "gardenize" the world.

Summary

◆ God ordained that we would have work from the beginning so we would participate in the development of the world.

◆ Even if we can get our work done quickly and make a good living, we should still find ways to advance the Dominion Mandate.

◆ Five common hindrances to work are: an entitlement mentality, feeling like a victim, laziness, procrastination, and amusements.

◆ Work is distinct from play in that it involves responsibility. Work is necessary to fulfill the purpose God has for you.

◆ Those who have made the greatest contributions to the world have not been afraid to take on work and responsibility.

◆ The work God gives you is a gift, and you find contentment as you realize your calling has come from His hand.

◆ A prime motivation for work should be to fulfill your part in the Dominion Mandate.

Make it Personal

1. What is your general attitude toward work?

2. What hindrances keep you from the work God has for you?

3. What motivates you in your work?

Chapter 7

Find Your Calling

There's Something the World Needs You to Be Doing

"But now God has placed the members, each one of them, in the body, just as He desired."
~ 1 Corinthians 12:18

People are used to the idea that certain individuals are called to the ministry. People are not as used to the concept that there are those also called to other areas of service. But it's in realizing people are called to all kinds of honorable work that you are able to discover your own calling in life.

A lot of people make a division between "secular" and "sacred" callings or activities. For the most part, this distinction isn't helpful. The world belongs to the Lord. So no matter how you find yourself occupied, it ought to be in service of the Lord.

Recalling the word "vocation" helps us understand this idea.

The word vocation, defined in Webster's Dictionary as "calling, employment, or occupation," is not used much anymore. It was once a common way to identify one's calling in the world. That calling usually coincided with the work a person did for a living. Though the word vocation has fallen out of use, the idea of being called to a particular purpose is still with us.

Coming to terms with what you've been called to do is vital when it comes to knowing your purpose in the world.

Basic Assumptions

Dissatisfaction runs high when it comes to what people are doing with their lives. There's a lot of coveting of other people's situations, too. A big reason for this is people often assume they need to be like someone else to be happy and successful. So they try and follow another person's path rather than pursue the course that's right for them.

If you are in that boat, I urge you to get out of it. You can't find your own calling if you are preoccupied with keeping up with someone else's.

The alternative is to adopt a new operating assumption. Reject the idea you need to be doing what someone else does and realize God has something uniquely suited to your life. There's a far greater likelihood you'll find your niche with this approach.

> God has something that you are uniquely suited to do with your life.

The idea of different people filling different roles is a long-established part of life. We can even see it in God Himself, and the way He operates. The three persons of the Trinity—Father, Son, and Holy Spirit—each have their own unique functions. There's no hint of jealousy among them, just recognition of each one's part.

Also, the church is known as the body of Christ, with each member of the body having its part (1 Cor. 12:12ff.). Here, too, there's no room for coveting another's place. Some parts of the body may be more visible and gain more recognition, but what counts is whether each member is faithful in his or her station.

This same principle of each person having a role to fill also applies in the world at large. It's the purpose of this chapter to help you find the place God has for you. If you are like many, you have no firm idea what you ought to do with your life. Or, you may have some idea, but are fuzzy on the details. In either case, there is much to be gained by learning more about the concept of "calling."

The Prerequisite To Finding Your Calling

This is important. To know what God is calling you to do with your life, you first need to know who you are as a person. *Knowing who you are comes before knowing what you should do.* This isn't meant to be a deep philosophical statement. It's just the way it is.

Coming to know who you are takes place as you are able to answer some basic questions about yourself: Do you know how God views you? Have you received His forgiveness? Do you know who you are in Jesus Christ? Are you honest with yourself as a person?

These issues are addressed in various ways throughout this book. (A summary of the restoration that is available to you is found in Appendix A.) As you interact with these issues, you are able to know your own identity, and are in a position to discover more specifically what God would have you do with your life.

97

How to Find Your Calling

Although finding your calling can't be reduced to a simple formula, two basic questions are helpful when you consider what your calling may be. What do you desire to do? What are you good at?

First, what do you want to do? What are you really interested in? What do you tend to gravitate toward? What is it you would keep doing whether you get paid or not?

What do you want to do?

What are you good at?

The Bible tells us for someone to be called to the office of elder, he first has to desire the position (1 Timothy 3:1). The same principle applies outside of the church, too.

Is there something you continually desire to do? Assuming, of course, it's ethical, your desire can be a good indicator you should be involved with it in one fashion or another.

The second question to consider is, what are you good at? What seems to come naturally or easy for you? What is it people praise and recognize you for? What seems to fit your character, temperament, and gifts?

The Bible also tells us to be qualified for the office of elder a man must show he is fit for the position, as confirmed by others (1 Timothy 3:2ff.).

If you are good at something, and others affirm it, it's likely you ought to be doing it in some way. The reason why you're good at anything is because God gave you gifts which are to be used and enjoyed.

NOTE: The Bible speaks of gifts in various places, like Romans 12:3-8 and 1 Peter 4:10, 11. The Scriptures also reveal how God gives us talents that we are to use to further His kingdom (Matthew 25:14-30).

In reflecting on these questions, ask others for insight. A spouse, parents, instructors, close friends, work associates and others can see areas you don't. Talk with them. It will help you more accurately evaluate yourself.

If you have an area of interest but are not good at it, it may indicate it's not the place for you. Or, you may not be as bad as you think, and only need further training and experience. Here's where the advice of others can help.

Don't forget to factor in your life history. God may have given you a variety of experiences that make the next step in your life more obvious. So consider how your experiences have helped shape you. Keep your eyes open to the ways God may have providentially prepared you for the opportunities before you now.

For many years my wife and I thought one of our sons was well-suited to work with computers. But he just didn't see it. Then one day he was thinking of finding new work and an opportunity with a computer company fell right in his lap. Suddenly, his eyes were opened to how right this was for him.

Finding the Right Fit
God has likely given you a variety of gifts and abilities. This can make finding where you fit more challenging. To decide how you should best use these, give thought to where your strongest propensities lie.

Bill Mouser is a seasoned pastor who has done excellent work regarding the makeup of men and women. In his materials, he identifies different aspects that distinguish a man and a woman's identity, as created by God.

For a man, besides being oriented towards dominion, he is made to be a cultivator who develops what's within his realm. He's a savior who brings healing or deliverance to the oppressed. He's a sage who presents wisdom and insight to those needing guidance. And, finally, he is one who reflects the glory of God.

For a woman, as well as being a companion in the dominion effort, she is a helper and completer. She is a life-giver, and a lady of wisdom. And she is one who enhances the glory of man as a crown does for a king.

Each of these aspects appears in every man or woman, but one or more may appear to be especially strong in a given person. These propensities can help point the way to a particular calling.

Here are a few examples of what I mean.

One who desires to venture into new territory could make a good land developer or researcher as he goes beyond the boundaries of what's familiar. One who is skilled in cultivating what is entrusted to him might be a good manager or supervisor. Someone who works well under stress to deliver others from trouble might make a good surgeon or rescue worker. He who has good insight and is able to guide others wisely could be suited as a counselor or coach. Someone with creative gifts can further God's glory as an artist, musician, or photographer.

As you evaluate your own leanings, consider how you can best serve others. After all, finding your own calling is as much about finding how you can best help other people as it is discovering what you're most cut out to do with your life.

Your Job and Calling

People sometimes wonder what to do when they have an idea what their calling is, but can't figure out how to make it support them financially.

Christian economist and author Gary North suggests the way to approach this is to make a distinction between your calling and your job.

Your calling is the unique contribution you bring to the world, which would be difficult to replace if you were gone. Your job is what you do to feed your family and pay the bills.

The ideal is to have both your calling and job perfectly coincide. This is worth striving to attain, but it may be difficult to accomplish, at least initially. You may need to be satisfied having your job pay the bills, and fulfill what you believe is your calling outside of your paid work.

This shouldn't discourage you.

Most people can find an overlap between their calling and job. Plus, your job is still a way to advance the Dominion Mandate. Every day you are on that job you should be discovering how you can serve the Lord better through it. As you develop yourself as a person—and are faithful where God has you—opportunities that better join your calling and job may arise.

But even if you never find yourself with a job that perfectly coincides with your calling, you shouldn't be disheartened, because your job can be the means to fulfill your calling in a significant way.

In the sixteenth century there was a merchant named Humphrey Monmouth. Most have never heard of him. Monmouth's job was to run a successful cloth company.

His calling, however, was something different. It was to provide room, board, and financial support for William Tyndale. More people have heard of Tyndale. His calling was to translate the Bible into English in the face of great opposition.

This story does more than show that some obscure callings are more important than we realize. It also shows that the ability of one person to fulfill his calling can be dependent on another being faithful in his. If Humphrey Monmouth would not have answered the call to help William Tyndale, it's likely the Bible would not have been translated to English until later, and maybe by someone other than Tyndale.

There are some people who have the same calling for many years, but accomplish that calling through different jobs. This has been true of my own situation. It's always been my calling to help others find their place in life, and assist them to be as faithful and fruitful as possible. For over twenty years I fulfilled this calling by working as a pastor, but now I fulfill it by helping others discover and implement their calling through my consulting and copywriting services.

As you seek to clarify what you believe you are being called to do with your life, there are a number of questions to ask yourself.

First, in what area do you believe you can make the greatest contribution? There are likely lots of areas you can contribute to fulfilling the Dominion Mandate, but maybe just one or two ways you know you could make a significant mark for God's kingdom.

Second, in what pursuit would you find yourself the most difficult to replace? Are you able or in a position to do something few others can? Do you have a perspective that's greatly needed? The way you answer questions like these can help you discern your calling.

Third, what kind of activity do you think you'll be able to look back on at the end of your life and believe it to be worthwhile? People are usually drawn to a particular calling because they believe it to be important. Try to project how you would view the calling you are considering at the end of your life. If you can imagine it being something of importance on your deathbed, it's worth investigating further.

Fourth, how can you best fulfill your calling and meet your financial needs? It's possible to have a calling that is able to provide financially. But if you're not finding a way to have your calling sustain you, see if there is a job that complements your calling.

Working through the process to discover your calling can be challenging. Be patient. By giving the attention to this it deserves, you are attending to one of the most important tasks imaginable—finding your place in life.

In Seth Godin's book, *Linchpin,* he makes the case that in today's economy it's not enough to be good at what you do. You need to become indispensable. The way to become indispensable is to become a problem solver, and a leader, who is able to chart a course without a map.

In one sense, of course, no one is ever indispensable because God can always choose to use someone else.

And, we know that people die and others take their place.

But in another sense, there are times when the role we play is essential, like that of Queen Esther when she faced the need to act to save her people.

For some readers, having an indispensable role may seem implausible. They simply can't envision doing anything more than a good job at what they've been told to do.

But what if we take seriously the concept that God has called us to do something? And what if it is clear that He has given the knowledge, experience, and opportunity to do what others cannot?

If people were to pay attention to these things, many would see themselves as indispensable, or at least called, and act on what God is showing them.

On a Mission From God

Once you come to terms with your calling, it's time to start fulfilling it. This may mean making changes. Maybe major changes, like quitting a job, getting additional training, or even relocating.

After some careful planning, start moving ahead. Don't over analyze. Don't delay. Don't snuff out your vision with lack of attention and unbelief. Even if you don't have a perfect plan, get started. Sometimes the information you need to refine your calling and how you'll get there will not become available until you're in motion.

Be sure and remember, even as you gain clarity about your calling you may still face obstacles in following it. Just because you have a calling doesn't mean it's going to be easy. Being aware that obstacles will come can help you persevere.

As you pursue your calling, work to keep yourself motivated. You'll need to "keep the vision," so to speak. The Lord Jesus has given you a mission that is part of accomplishing His purpose in the world.

Remembering these truths will help you.

Everything you have is a gift. God has given you certain capabilities. These are not to be wasted, but used to further His kingdom in the unique place He has called you. There may be others with similar gifts and circumstances, but no one is more right for the task God led you to than you.

God gives you authority to do what He desires. The fact you are alive shows God has something for you to do, and it's a good possibility what He has in mind is more significant than what you've done so far. Once you discover what it is, don't hold back. Be inspired, confident, and get busy doing it, knowing He stands behind you.

Be a faithful steward. God has given you a portion of the world to rule. No matter how big or small your realm may be, give careful attention to rule it well. Give far less attention to how others are doing managing their realms. When the day of reckoning comes, you won't have to give an account for how well others ruled their realms. Just how well you ruled over yours.

As you come to the place where you have a sense of mission about your calling, you will have a purpose for living like few others. This is a good reason to always keep your calling clear.

Know Your Boundaries, Sharpen Your Focus

I'm always saddened when people waste their lives. Those who squander their years through drugs or other addictive problem are obvious examples. But there are other, not so obvious examples, too.

I'm thinking of the numbers of people with a vision of what they're to be doing with their lives. They also had an idea of how the vision can be fulfilled and were motivated to get started, but never persisted to accomplish anything of significance in that direction.

Be wary. Once you get clarity on what you're supposed to be doing, you must take care to see it through. Many distractions will come to derail you on your journey. Sometimes distractions will come disguised as opportunities from people who mean to do you well, but they haven't done the work of zeroing in on your calling as you have.

To protect yourself, take measures to stay true to your calling.

One important way is to set boundaries for yourself. Be careful who you listen to. Don't be afraid to say no. If necessary, avoid certain people or situations. This may seem drastic or unkind, but remember, it's your calling you're responsible for. Fear God more than men.

Another way to protect yourself is to continually focus on what you are pursuing. As you begin to implement your calling, you will have a general idea where you are headed. As you work at it and gain experience, your focus will become clearer, narrower and deeper. As it does, you will become more effective.

Finally, as you grow in your calling, stay connected with others who have experience and expertise that can sharpen you and keep you on track. Protecting yourself from the voices that may distract you does not mean you should shut yourself off from the influence of others. That would be a big mistake that inhibits your growth.

When you work hard at being true to your calling, your sense of purpose will keep on growing. And your usefulness for God's kingdom will keep growing too.

In whatever God calls you to do—no matter how mundane or insignificant it may seem—you are to please Him through faithful service.

Trust in the Lord and do good; dwell in the land and cultivate faithfulness. ~ Psalm 37:3

Summary

◆ The distinction that's sometimes made between "sacred" and "secular" can cause us to forget the world belongs to the Lord, and every occupation should be done in His service.

◆ The word "vocation" carries the idea that people are

called to many lines of work.

◆ To find your own calling, stop coveting the calling of another, and believe God has something uniquely suited for your life.

◆ The prerequisite to finding your calling is to know who you are in the Lord.

◆ There are two questions to answer when considering your calling. What do you want to do? What are you good at?

◆ Discovering your calling involves consideration of how you can best contribute to the lives of others.

◆ Your job and calling may not be the same. It is wise to have them overlap as much as possible.

◆ As you come to terms with your calling, pursue it as one on a mission from God. As you take action, you're calling will likely be refined and made clear.

Make it Personal

1. What do you want to do with your life?

2. What have others confirmed you are good at?

3. What direction would lead you to make the greatest contribution to the lives of others?

Chapter 8

Stay Faithful

Your Success Requires It

". . . what does the Lord require of you, but to fear the Lord your God, to walk in all His ways and love Him, and to love the Lord your God with all your heart and all your soul, and to keep the Lord's commandments and His statutes which I am commanding you today for good?
~Deuteronomy 10:12, 13

There are many people today who want success more than anything else in life. They want it so badly they will cut ethical corners because they believe they must to succeed. But the irony is, to really succeed you must maintain your integrity.

To understand the irony at play in this you may need to adjust your beliefs about what makes one a success.

What is Success?
What is it to be a success? How you answer will make a difference in how your life unfolds, so think about this carefully.

Start by thinking about who the world regards as a success. It's the ones with money and power. It's those who are popular and get a lot of acclaim. It's the people who have lived life the way they want to.

But are these people really successful?

It depends on how you define success.

The world defines success according to certain criteria like money, power, influence, and sex appeal. These criteria *may* go along with a truly successful life, but they aren't reliable indicators because God's definition of success is different.

For Him, being a success is to have His favor. It's to be faithful to one's calling and responsibilities. It's to live with Him and others in peace, both now and in eternity.

These are not criteria the world appreciates, but they are the criteria that lead to success before God. As well as the blessing that goes with it.

The reason there are two sets of criteria is that there are two kingdoms vying for your allegiance—the kingdom of God and the kingdom of mammon. Each kingdom has its own master. With one it is God, and the other it is the stuff of this world. Having one of these masters rule you is unavoidable. You are either ruled by God or the passing things of this world.

What can be confusing is that some signs of success can overlap kingdoms. Wealth is a sign of success in the kingdom of mammon. But it also can be an indicator of blessing in the kingdom of God.

The fact that wealth can indicate success in either kingdom can be dangerous. It can cause you to assume you are right with God when you're really not. It can also send you in pursuit of the sign of blessing instead of the

One who blesses, which can bring you into bondage to mammon.

There's a much safer and secure way. It's to follow God, and allow Him to bless as He sees fit. That blessing may or may not involve wealth and power and so on. But that's alright. He knows what's best for you.

It's About Ethics

For most, the way to succeed is to use your intelligence and energy to make a name for yourself.

> Finding success is really about aligning yourself with God and His purpose for you in the world.

Working smart is good, as is gaining a reputation in your area of calling. But if this is all you've got, you will come up short.

The route to success is about more than using your wits and mastering the art of self-promotion. These may give worldly success for a time, but they don't deliver the kind of success that makes for a life well-lived. Only knowing you've lived as God wants you to can do that.

Finding success is really about aligning yourself with God and His purpose for you in the world.

As we've already seen, God created the world and all that is in it. Because God made us, He set the terms for how we are to live. He is the one who makes the rules. How well we follow the rules affects how well it goes for us. Obedience leads to blessing and disobedience leads to judgment. Those who submit to His word as a way of life are the ones who inherit the earth.

113

This was God's design from the beginning. Adam was impatient with the design, and he suffered due to his disobedience. Christ lived a life of patient obedience and inherited the earth. Jesus showed us how to live in keeping with the design. Those who trust Him become joint heirs with Him.

Since the 1992 presidential election, political strategists have used the phrase "It's the economy, stupid" to bring focus to their candidate's campaign. When it comes to winning elections, it's probably still a message worth focusing on.

But when it comes to winning God's favor, we can't lose sight of the fact it's all about ethics and we're stupid if we ignore this. God still blesses obedience and curses disobedience. When nations deny Him, it turns out badly. Our real strength—or weakness—depends on our spiritual condition.

Living by God's Standard

Because God chose to bless those who trust Him and live by His standard, it's important to know what that standard is.

Throughout civilization, the Ten Commandments have served as a summary of God's standard for humanity. These commandments were given to God's people after they were delivered from Egypt. Because they were given after the deliverance, their purpose was never to provide a way of salvation. Their purpose was—and is—to show us how to live and experience His blessing.

Today, we have not only the Ten Commandments, but all of God's Word to serve as our rule. This standard has served humanity well, and provided the foundation for what's known as Western Civilization.

Here's one example of how God's standard has served us.

The eighth commandment, "thou shall not steal," assumes the right to acquire and hold private property. That's because you can't steal what is not already owned by someone else (Ex.20:15). With the protection this commandment provides, there's an incentive to be productive. Because you know the fruit of your labor will be yours and protected. But without the protection this commandment provides, the motivation for productive labor is taken away. There's no longer assurance the fruit of your labor will be preserved. The nation that forsakes this rule guts the productive spirit of the people. Eventually, it will be filled with those who make their living by plundering others.

I trust you've noticed that our own nation is already far down this path. Excessive taxation, currency inflation, and fraud are all forms of stealing, and have us on a path we can't afford to stay on much longer.

When God's Word is obeyed, it brings blessings to individuals, families, churches, and society as a whole. But when the standard of God's Word is ignored, it brings confusion, and the withdrawal of God's favor.

God's Word emphasizes that obedience brings His blessing. When we are careful to meditate on God's precepts so that we would do them, we'll find we prosper and have success. This is God's principle. Even if the institutions of our nation have rejected this principle, you should not. Your security is found in trusting and obeying God, even while others don't.

Important Point: None of this talk of needing to obey God's standard diminishes the place of His grace.   The only way to receive God's favor is by His grace.   That never changes.   Yet, God gives His law as an expression of His grace.   Because it's in abiding by His standard we find the way to experience His blessings further.

The World's Success

Here's a logical question: If God blesses obedience and curses disobedience, why does it seem like there are many unbelievers who get along just fine while faithful believers struggle and suffer?

I'll answer the question about the hardship believers suffer in the next chapter, and take up the apparent blessing experienced by unbelievers here.

There are several ways to explain the fact that unbelievers can seem to do well, even though they don't live for the Lord.

First, there is God's love for His creation.   By God's common grace He sends rain on the just and the unjust. This means even those who do not acknowledge God as the source of every good gift benefit from His kindness, and are able to use the gifts God provides to further their own agendas for a time.

Second, throughout history unbelievers have often attained certain accomplishments before believers do. They seem to get there first.   This goes way back.   For example, Cain, a murderer, was the first to build a city.

The thought of unbelievers achieving as they do might cause some distress, but it shouldn't.   God has a plan even for the gains of the unrighteous.

The Bible tells us "the wealth of the wicked is being laid up for the righteous" (Proverbs 13:22). So, even though ungodly men may amass a fortune, in the end its title will be transferred to those who are joint heirs with Christ. A pretty humbling thought.

Finally, the unrighteous often use their power to set up systems to profit themselves at the expense of others. This arrangement allows them to accumulate riches for a season. The prophet Amos rebuked this practice when the power brokers of his day oppressed the righteous for their own gain. Similar corruption infects many of those who are in high places today.

Prosperity acquired this way seems like it will be held in the hands of the wicked forever, but eventually it will take wings.

So, when you look on the unrighteous in their prosperity, don't despair, be covetous or fear. Scripture makes it plain their downfall will come. They'll be mowed down like grass. Instead of fretting, keep your eyes on the Lord and your hands devoted to the calling He has given you (Psalm 37:1-3).

Long-Term Thinking
There are plenty of short-term thinkers who are always looking for a way to make a quick buck. People like this somehow amaze others by their ability to escape their own ruin and experience luxuries coveted by others.

But these people never will be really successful. They are too fixated on the signs of success, and not patient enough to wait for the results of a calling faithfully pursued. On the outside they may have the look of success, but if you could peer inside, you'd find a lot of fear and uncertainty.

What's needed is a long-term view. This is true for individuals, and for societies.

God takes His time working in people's lives so they can be ready for what He has in mind for them. He's not in a hurry, even though we are. Patient trust along with active obedience will never fail you. It may be hard to see in the short-term, but in the long-term it's always true.

> God takes His time working in people's lives so they will be prepared for what He has in mind for them.

As a culture is faithful, there is a shared ethic that builds up and this brings multiplied blessings. This is how civilizations are established—with long-term thinking.

In previous generations this viewpoint was apparent in the way buildings were constructed. They were built over years with stones and other materials meant to last. We don't see that often today.

The way to develop a long-term vision is to have the vision the Bible provides become a part of you. This is why reading the Bible regularly is such an important habit.

When Blessing Comes

With patience and obedience comes increasing success. Usually, some level of prosperity will show up with it. **When this blessing comes, don't forget where it came from.**

In Scripture there is a destructive pattern repeated over and over. It goes like this. . . God's people suffer under oppression. They turn to the Lord for relief and follow Him. They are faithful, and it leads to blessing. And they are blessed with abundance. Then, what do they do? They forget the Lord.

They say, "My power and the might of my hand have gotten me this wealth" (Deuteronomy 8:17). Then they forsake His commandments, because they don't think they need Him anymore.

It's this pride that afflicts our own generation so severely, but don't let it afflict you. The way to avoid it is two-fold.

First, remember, the more God blesses you, the more responsibility you have. Go ahead and enjoy what God gives you with a thankful heart, but don't kick back and spend it all on your own pleasures. God blesses so you would be in a position to do more for His kingdom. Discover what that is, and go after it.

Second, always live in the fear of the Lord. The fear of the Lord leads to wisdom, obedience and success. Always remember God has mercifully given you all you have. This will help protect you from the pride and worldliness that keeps so many from succeeding during their earthly lives.

Pursue success in what God has called you to do. Be assured God wants you to succeed because He's called you, and desires your efforts to advance the Dominion Mandate as much as possible. He's given you the guidelines to make it happen. They're found in the principles of His Word.

Just never forget the source of your success once you achieve it.

People often wonder, can I be a success and still maintain my integrity? Actually, living with integrity is the only way to have success.

Summary

◆ To really succeed you have to maintain your integrity, because God views success in terms of faithfulness to one's calling and responsibilities.

◆ There are two kingdoms vying for our allegiance: the kingdom of God and the kingdom of mammon. Wealth can be a sign of success in either kingdom, so we must be wary.

◆ God blesses obedience and curses disobedience. Over the long run, those who submit to His Word inherit the earth.

◆ When God's Word has been obeyed through history, it has led to cultural development and wealth creation.

◆ God may allow the unrighteous to prosper for a season because of His common grace, but their wealth is being laid up for the righteous.

◆ Patient trust and active obedience never fail.

◆ When success is achieved, the pride of self-sufficiency must be avoided. We must continually live with humble reliance on the Lord.

Make it Personal

1. How do you define success?

2. In what areas do you need to pay more attention to abiding by God's standard?

3. In what ways can you demonstrate that God is the source of your success?

Chapter 9

Trust Your Way Through Trials

God is at Work in Them

"And we know that God causes all things to work together for good to those who love God, to those who are called according to His purpose."
~ Romans 8:28

Personal trials are aggravating. They seem like such a waste. We think to ourselves, "If it weren't for that financial setback, we'd really be well off." Or, "If I hadn't have gotten sick, I'd be so much further ahead."

Reflections like these seem plausible, but they assume an awful lot. Mainly, they assume we know better than God what's best for us. That's not a smart assumption to make. God knows better than we do. The Old Testament story of Joseph assures us of this (Genesis 37-50).

There's much about Joseph's life we can identify with. And there's a lot it can teach us about trusting God through our trials, too.

Joseph was born into a family filled with promise. He was the favored son of his father, Jacob, and had a lot going for him, but his life was far from easy.

Joseph's brothers were jealous of him. They almost killed him, but instead sold him into slavery. While a slave in Egypt, Joseph fulfilled his duty faithfully. This brought blessing to Joseph, and his master. But then Joseph was falsely accused by his master's wife, causing him to spend years in an Egyptian prison.

While in prison, Joseph continued as a faithful servant, which was part of his character. He devoted himself to doing his duty the best he could. During this time, it became apparent that Joseph was blessed with extraordinary wisdom.

Finally, Joseph's reputation for wisdom enabled him to get out of prison. The pharaoh needed advice, and Joseph was called upon for his supernatural insight. His counsel to the pharaoh was so remarkable he made Joseph the prime minister of Egypt.

Soon a famine came to the whole region of Egypt, but thanks to Joseph's insight, the nation was prepared. Because of Joseph's provisions, other nations came to Egypt for food, including Joseph's brothers. In this way God provided for the family of Jacob and preserved His people Israel.

Throughout Joseph's hardships, he showed no signs of bitterness. He kept giving his all in the place God had him, and God blessed him for his patient trust. Even Joseph's brothers expected him to be vindictive toward them. But he wasn't, because he trusted completely in God. He was able to say to his brothers, "As for you, you meant evil against me, but God meant it for good. . ." (Genesis 50:20).

God's Providence

The God who worked in Joseph's life is the same God who

124

works in your life and mine. God hasn't changed. As He used trials to bring good out of bad a few millennia ago, so is He able to do today.

The particular aspect of God's character that moves Him to work in this purposeful way is known as His providence.

The best definition of providence ever given is found in a historic creed known as the Westminster Confession of Faith. The first paragraph of this definition reads:

> God, the great Creator of all things, doth uphold, direct, dispose, and govern all creatures, actions, and things, from the greatest even to the least, by his most wise and holy providence, according to his infallible foreknowledge, and the free and immutable counsel of his own will, to the praise of the glory of his wisdom, power, justice, goodness, and mercy.

Although some of the language of this statement is archaic, the substance is plain. God is involved in every detail of our lives. He knows what He's doing, and He is working for your good. Even in times of hardship.

God's providence reminds us He is in control of every disappointment and setback we face.

Reflecting on God's providence brings confidence and hope. It reminds us we don't live in an impersonal world, where we're mere victims of random forces. We're part of a world ruled by a personal God who governs everything according to His wise purpose.

In God's providence there will be times we find our lives drastically

125

altered—by sickness, death of loved ones, job losses, financial reversals, betrayals, and more. Through it all, God still rules and intentionally works out His purpose.

God's providence reminds us He is in control of every disappointment and setback we face. During such times, we must remember the refrain of Psalm 136 which says, "His lovingkindness is everlasting." In this we find our peace.

Your Plans and God's
Even though God is providentially at work in our hardships, most of us still find trials upsetting. Why do we have such a hard time resigning ourselves to the fact God is doing something different than we expected?

It comes down to realizing we have our plans, and God has His.

Whether written or not, we have our own plans with personal goals and agendas. There's nothing wrong with this. Goals and agendas are how things get done.

But our plans can be a problem if they're inflexible and unable to adjust to unexpected changes God brings. When our goals and agendas are rigid, we see obstacles that come our way as threats instead of course changes directed by God.

The remedy for this is to trust Jesus and always put faithfulness to God first.

Of course, we'll never know all the details of God's plan. And there are parts we only come to know as His plan unfolds. But His basic purpose has been made clear.

He's out to see His Dominion Mandate fulfilled.

As we've seen, getting this mandate fulfilled involves people like you. People with individual gifts and talents, hopes and dreams.

But to be in the best position to play your part in this mission, you need the kind of character God can use to make the most of your efforts. God knows this, and it's why He's at work in your life.

Don't forget that God's plans are bigger than yours. He sees the big picture, and knows how you can best fit in. Don't fight the work He's doing in your life. Be thankful for it.

God is Serious About Your Maturity

God's goal for human beings has always been that they live a life of maturity. His plan is for us to trust Him and receive His blessings with gratitude, and use them responsibly to further His kingdom.

Adam failed at this, setting the mold for all who came after him. Being Adam's sons and daughters, we all lack the kind of maturity God intends for us. But God sent Jesus Christ as a new Adam. **As the new Adam, Jesus lived as a mature man, and fulfilled His calling perfectly so we would be able to fulfill ours.**

Growing in maturity is a process. A process that involves hardship.

Nobody wants hardship any more than they want to change a flat tire on the expressway in the rain, but God uses hardship to test, teach, and strengthen us.

Hardship has a way of helping you to see things you didn't see before. It brings past lessons into clearer focus. This improved sight brings depth of character when we're open to learn what God is teaching us.

It's through this process God works to bring us to maturity. This is why it's always good to be prayerful when under trials. Ask the Lord, "What do you want me to see?" And, "Where do I need to change?"

As you submit to the Lord over time, your maturity will increase (emphasis on *as you submit*).

> Maturity does not come automatically with age.

Maturity does not come automatically with age. It comes as we submit to God and accept reality as He made it.

As you do mature, your ability to be used by God grows. So, to make the most of your life, it makes sense to make maturity a goal for your life, just as God does.

Marks of Maturity

Since growing in maturity is so important, pay attention and monitor your progress in this area. One way to assess your progress is with these "marks of maturity."

How well does your life line up with these indicators?

You are patient instead of grasping. A mature person is able to rest in God's plan as it unfolds. He trusts God to grant what He will in His own time.

You value what God values. A sure sign of growth in maturity is when you value less of what is superficial and more of what has been revealed as important by God.

You live with dependence on God. Those who are

immature seek to bring an end to any given trial so they can get back to living independently from God. The mature seek to use their trials to grow in dependence on Him.

You have a greater concern about wisdom than appearance. A reliable mark of maturity is you're more concerned about living wisely than looking good to others.

You make a habit of replacing pride with humility. The spiritually mature person is continually learning he doesn't have all the answers—and he doesn't pretend to either. He knows God is opposed to the proud but gives grace to the humble, and acts accordingly.

You are dedicated to serving others before yourself. He who is mature has died to himself and been made alive to the needs of others. He makes it his practice to put others first.

You conduct yourself with a grateful attitude. The more you mature, the more you realize everything you have has been given to you as a gift of God's grace. And what you have is better than you deserve.

Your life exhibits the fruit of God's Spirit. This fruit of the Spirit includes love, joy, peace, patience, kindness, goodness, faithfulness, gentleness, and self-control. You can't have maturity without it.

By regularly holding your life up to these marks, you'll find you have an imperfect but useful way to gauge your growth. So consider them often.

Growth in spiritual maturity involves both God's initiative and our response. It is not something we can speed up on our own timetable. It comes about slowly but surely as we submit to the Lord in pursuit of Christlikeness.

At the end of life there is little that can be more satisfying than knowing you've submitted yourself to the process of spiritual growth God has had for you. And because of it, you lived the most fruitful life possible.

What does it mean to wait on the Lord?

It means trusting in His goodness. It means being open to receive what He has for you. It means being content with His timing. It means living with confident expectation of His provision.

When we wait on the Lord, we express our dependence on Him. We acknowledge that He is the One who sets the terms.

Waiting on the Lord is not passive. It watches. It prays. It meditates. It obeys. It serves.

Life Stages

Maturity involves working oneself through certain stages, from childhood through adulthood. Each of these stages comes with certain temptations, and as we pass the tests involved in one stage, we move on to the next.

Growing up involves more than physical maturation. Just because someone turns 21 or 50 or has gray hair does not mean he's wise and mature.

There's a need to work through each stage and learn the lessons God has planned.

It's in moving through these life stages with an awareness that God's work is being done that we mature and become those who can function as fully as God intends. Unfortunately, most people try to dodge the tests God has for them. And because of it, they never fully grow up to be what God has in mind for them.

Theologians have long noted that man fills the role of a priest, king, and prophet. More recently, biblical scholar James Jordan has pointed out these match the phases of a man's life. So, there is a progression from priest, to king, to prophet.

None of these roles should be confused with the actual office of a king of a country or priest in a church. Rather, they refer to one's position in life.

Each of these roles has something to do with one's relationship to authority.

When a man is young, he fulfills a priestly function. He comes to know the parameters of his calling, and how to submit himself to authority. He learns to guard and preserve what's been entrusted to him.

As a man reaches middle age, he craves something more. This includes more influence and authority.

To prepare a man for greater authority, God puts him through tests. The tests typically involve accepting less at the very time he wants more. For example, a man at work may be faced with the choice of acting unethically and getting a promotion or acting righteously and losing his job. This is a real test. And God is behind it, to see if the man is ready for greater authority.

This traumatic experience of wanting more at a time you're getting less is what's often referred to as a mid-life crisis. Those who fail the test often end up ruining their lives and the relationships with those close to them. Those who pass the test advance to a new stage in life, where there is greater authority and responsibility. This role is described as kingly, because it involves using this newly given authority and responsibility to rule some area with wisdom.

Those who serve well in the kingly phase may be raised up by God to the role of a prophet. This would be one who lives at the highest level of maturity, having close intimacy with God and a platform to speak and act on His behalf.

The focus here is that each stage of life involves its tests—and with them come opportunities to trust God. When you pass these tests, you become qualified to fill a larger purpose and complete your calling more fully.

Working through the stages of life can be among the more traumatic experiences you'll have to endure. You may feel like you're dying. And in a way you are, as God is making you into someone new.

Patience and Perspective

To benefit from the trials that God oversees in your life, you need patience. But patience is not something you can easily muster up at will. So how do you become more patient? By paying attention to your perspective on what's going on in your life.

As a child of Adam, your natural perspective is to view yourself as the center of all that happens in the world. From this vantage point, everything that occurs is viewed as either a help or a hindrance to achieving your goals.

Since life is filled with difficulties, the natural man often finds himself on the defensive as he seeks to deal with the challenges facing him. This way of life is not only stressful; it stunts personal development, and makes it very difficult for you to discover God's calling on your life.

For the person who lives by trusting God's grace, the situation is different. His perspective, though not perfectly clear, has God at the center, and himself in the orbit of what God is doing in the world.

With this view of life, your difficulties are seen less as personal threats and more as problems to solve and grow from. Here, you have a reduced level of stress and greater strength. And with this perspective you are able to enjoy consistent spiritual growth.

To sum up, the way to more patience is to fix your eyes on Jesus.

Realize, too, that you and your plans aren't as big a deal as you make them. God and His plans are a much bigger deal.

This does not mean God doesn't care about us in our trials. We know He does, because He sent His Son to suffer injustice, cruelty, and death to give us life in His new creation.

Summary

- ◆ Our trials are not a waste. God uses them.

- ◆ The Old Testament story of Joseph is full of lessons. The biggest lesson is that God providentially extends His lovingkindness.

- ◆ Realizing that God often interrupts our plans to further His own can help us to better endure hardships.

◆ God desires us to increase in maturity, and He uses the opportunities that hardship provides to bring about our growth.

◆ Patience is an important indicator of maturity.

◆ Each stage of life brings its tests. Middle-age, in particular, brings opportunities to prove our readiness to advance from priestly to kingly roles.

◆ We grow in patience as we realize that God is working out His purpose in our lives, and that His plans are bigger than our plans.

Make it Personal

1. In what experiences can you recognize God's providence at work?

2. What tests are you undergoing at present?

3. How might your response to your tests help or hinder you when it comes to living out your purpose?

Chapter 10

Don't Forget People

They are Part of God's Design

". . . for the one who does not love his brother whom he has seen, cannot love God whom he has not seen."
~ 1 John 4:20

If you are occupied trying to figure out what God wants you to do with your life, you can easily end up isolating yourself—and in the process become so absorbed with yourself you forget about people.

This is a mistake you need to avoid.

Who is it God uses to accomplish the Dominion Mandate? People. Who do you need to become all you can be in the world? Other people. And who are you to serve in this life in order to fulfill your purpose? Again, the answer is people.

No doubt, people can be a source of aggravation. There are times we all want to withdraw, but people are a big deal to God, and always will be. So don't ignore them as you work out your own place in the Dominion Mandate.

If you want to fulfill your purpose in life, you must realize other people will have a significant part to play. You need them, and they need you. I have more to say about this a little later in this chapter.

There is one God in three persons—Father, Son, and Holy Spirit. The fellowship among the persons of the Trinity helps us understand the important place people have in God's design for the world. It is this personal nature of God that also leads Him to call us to fellowship with Him and share in His plan for dominion in the world.

A Larger Mission

When you fixate on what you're doing with your life, it's easy to start thinking your gig is more important than anyone else's. But keep it in perspective. You, and all that occupies you, are part of a much larger plan. It's a significant part, but a small one in the overall scheme of things.

God's program does not involve you being consumed with your importance or achievements. It's about discovering the place He has for you, and how you can contribute to the lives of others. Then going ahead and applying yourself with everything you have.

Unless you fall under some exception I can't think of, there is some way your role relates to improving the lives of others.

That's worth devoting some extra thought to. Here's why.

People have a lot of hatred for one another today. And even where there's not hatred, most of us want to avoid being bothered by people. This has to do with more than just the fact that we're selfish. It has to do with people being made in God's image. So, just as people don't want to be bothered by God in their lives, neither do they want to be bothered by those who are made in His likeness.

If this is how you regard people, you'll want to stop and think about it. For one, it's a reflection of your relationship with God. If you can't give people whom you see their due, you won't give God whom you can't see His due. Disregarding people also says a lot about where you are in fulfilling your purpose, because the only way you can live out God's purpose for your life is in the service of people.

This does not mean you have to be surrounded by people all the time. Some of us are more introverted by nature, and there are many who serve others through solitary activities. What matters is that you're not hesitant to involve yourself in some way for the good of others, and that you do your work with an eye not only to serve God, but your fellow human beings.

> You can't serve God without serving those who are made in His image.

God designed His creation so that His image bearers would be important to us. You really can't serve Him without serving those made in His image.

Marriage

The relationship that has the greatest impact on fulfilling your purpose is your marriage. I know, not everyone is married, and it is possible to have a full and meaningful life while single, but the norm is marriage.

There's an obvious reason for this. God intends for children to be born and nurtured to maximum fruitfulness through marriage. That's His way of filling the earth and multiplying those who would rule over it.

There are less obvious reasons your marriage is so important to fulfilling your part in the Dominion Mandate, too. One of these is the benefit of companionship.

Companionship is more than having somebody to do something with. It's also the most natural way to find regular encouragement, and bring about your personal development.

The best opportunities you will have as a person to discover your weaknesses and overcome them is through marriage. The intimacy of the marriage relationship allows no hiding places. Sooner or later the truth about you will be revealed. This can be painful, but when you willingly accept it, you will find unending opportunities to grow.

A natural outcome is that those who are married normally fair better than those who aren't. This is particularly the case with men, as noted years ago by George Gilder, author of the classic book *Men and Marriage*. When men have a helpmate, and the obligations of a household, they advance further in their callings. They are healthier and wealthier, and society as a whole benefits as a result.

This is not to say those who are single or divorced are inferior or unable to make a contribution. Not at all. The point is: if you are married, you ought to value your marriage and make the most of it. It's filled with opportunities to make you a better person and increase the good you bring to the world.

This should be an encouragement to those who are afraid of getting married. Yes, marriage has its challenges. But for the vast majority, it is God's way for us to develop and be positioned to best fulfill our role in the Dominion Mandate.

Children

Despite all the talk about caring for children, our society tends to view them as a nuisance. The cost they require in terms of money, time, and attention has led many to see children as a curse instead of a blessing.

This isn't surprising in light of all the selfish and short-term thinking around. Sure, children will cost you, but in other ways they will make you rich like nothing else can.

Children will teach you lessons about yourself and life that are difficult to learn any other way. Sometimes this is uncomfortable, as you see your flaws fleshed out before you. But even when this occurs, it has its benefits. Being forced to face undeniable truths about yourself motivates you to change.

Children are also one of the best ways to extend your God-given mission in the world. As children are instructed and brought up to embrace a vision for fulfilling the Dominion Mandate, you are able to pass on a legacy that extends itself for generations.

Thinking beyond the present generation doesn't happen much anymore. We're too taken up with getting by today. This is apparent from the huge sum of debt our society has taken on—which will have to be dealt with in some way by our children and grandchildren.

But those who develop a vision for the Dominion Mandate realize it's a long-term project. They're able to think beyond their own generation to the next. And it's this vision that enables parents and the rest of society to make the sacrifices necessary to equip children for productive adulthood.

This preparation goes beyond the necessary academic training most expect. It includes character training, and awareness that they, too, have a place in the Dominion Mandate.

To bring this about takes deliberate, self-conscious effort. Effort you instinctively may not want to put forth, but the kind necessary for your children to get in their own hearts what their lives are all about.

A worthy goal for any parents is to create a covenant dynasty through your children that will bring Christ's dominion to the world, from one generation to the next.

Children, in most cases, will provide you with the best opportunity you'll have to make a positive mark on the future. Don't ignore the opportunity while you have it.

You Need People

It should be evident that people need to be a part of your life. In part because this is God's design to develop the world, but also because you need them.

Despite the glamour given to individualism and the idea of self-made men, no one makes it entirely on his or her own. Yes, you need to supply your motivation. Plus ideas, commitment, and work. But these alone will not get you to where you should be. You need the sharpening effect of others to achieve all God has for you.

The world is filled with proud and uncaring people who purposefully cut themselves off from others. There are also those whose fears and insecurities drive them to the safety of an isolated life, instead of one that calls for personal engagement. It may be said, "to each his own," but the sad reality is those who choose such an existence miss out on the kind of interaction and relationships needed to fully develop their humanity.

God planned for us to live in community. The model for this is the church, and the division of labor which exists in the body of Christ. As this takes place among God's people, it is to be followed as a model for society as a whole.

> It's amazing what even one new relationship can do to change your outlook and improve your situation.

This means you may need to come out of your shell to become what God intends for you. You may need to go out of your way to meet and be with more people. It's amazing what even one new relationship can do to change your outlook and improve your situation.

For some people this is a difficult area, and their state of isolation has become desperate. If you are in this category, commit yourself to take just one small step to get yourself out of it. That step may be to just say "hello" to someone you don't know. Then take another step. And keep taking steps until you have a growing network of friends and acquaintances God can use to refine you and guide you.

You simply cannot fulfill the purpose God has in mind for you without the involvement of others. So don't allow yourself to get isolated. Make sure you find ways to get in circulation with people and stay connected with them.

"The ministry would be great if it weren't for the people."
It's a line many pastors have used in jest, but it brings up
an important question for all of us.

Where would you be without people?

What would you and your life be like? What kind of
family would you have? And what about friends? Who
would your clients, customers, or patients be?

It's a given that dealing with people brings hassles, but
dealing with people is what life is about. Get that point
settled, and you'll be a big step ahead when it comes to
realizing your purpose.

People Need You

Another group of people who are detached from others is
made up of those who see themselves as insignificant, and
with little to offer.

People like this commonly endure long periods of
loneliness. They're often bored and depressed as they fail
to see any real purpose for their lives. In the worst cases,
people in this situation are suicidal. Sadly, this number is
growing.

Some of the most important words that can be said to a
person trapped in this scenario are: "You have something
to offer, and people need you."

Everyone has something to contribute to the world. And

God has a place for each one. He desires everyone to find and develop what he has to offer for the benefit of others. By His grace, this is possible for anyone in any situation.

Those who feel useless and depressed usually find themselves there because at some point something went wrong for them. Maybe their efforts weren't appreciated. Or they felt they tried to bring good to others, but it never worked out as intended. They are convinced nothing works for them, so they give up. And when they do, they're usually left with feelings of bitterness and resentment.

The way people get to this place is not hard to understand, but it's not a place to stay. It's a place of self-pity and sorrow that only leads one on a downward spiral.

To reverse this spiral you need to focus on doing good wherever you have the opportunity. Even if it doesn't seem like much, you need to step out and do it. And you must remember it's not up to you to force any result. God's the one who brings results. Our responsibility is to give our best to the assignment He gives us.

Remember, too, feelings of self-worth do not come from the approval of others. If that's where you are looking for them, you will be disappointed. The only place to find your worth as a person is to realize you've been made by God to do the works He has given you to do. Do them, and leave the results to Him.

"It is more blessed to give than receive."
~ Acts 20:35

A Life of Service

The connection between being involved with people and finding your purpose is found in the word "service." In one way or another, your life is to be about serving others.

It was the new Adam, the one who brings redemption, that said He "did not come to be served, but to serve, and to give His life a ransom for many" (Mk.10:45). This selfless service is to be a model for us. We know this because He also said whoever wishes to be great is to be a servant of all (Mk. 9:35).

> The connection between being involved with people and finding your purpose is found in the word "service."

Service requires sacrifice. It involves turning away from yourself to the purpose God has for you. Though it runs counter to your natural desires, this is how you arrive at the best life God has for you. It's the one who loses his life in His service that finds it (Mt.16:25).

By the way, in my many years as a counselor I discovered the best way for someone to get out of a funk is to get out and serve somebody. I believe I shared this advice more than any other. And it worked practically every time I gave it.

Service is God's way for you to bring value to the world and advance the Kingdom. Those who serve best are given greater authority, and find themselves with more opportunities to do good. Authority is not given to anyone to gain advantages for himself, but to be a greater blessing to others.

Once you discover the relationship between service and

your purpose in life, your attitude toward people changes. It goes from seeing others as obstacles, irritations, and objects to be used, to those who are essential to your reason for living.

It's for this reason, it is more blessed to give than receive (Acts 20:35). Because it's in serving others you find your purpose.

Summary

◆ When you are taken up with refining your calling, you can end up isolating yourself. This is a hazard to avoid.

◆ In some way or another, your mission in life will involve people. How you regard people will affect your readiness for the role God has for you.

◆ Your marriage relationship will have the greatest impact on how well you fulfill your purpose in the world.

◆ Normally, children provide one of the best opportunities you'll have to make a positive mark on the future.

◆ You need people to maximize your own development as a person.

◆ People need what you have to offer the world, even if it seems insignificant in your eyes.

◆ Your attitude toward people changes as you remember that God calls you to use the gifts He's given you to serve others.

Make it Personal

1. What is your view of people, and how do your actions reflect that view?

2. In what ways do you see your relationship with your spouse and children preparing you to be further used by God?

3. What keeps you from serving others more than you do?

Chapter 11

Rule Yourself First

How Can You Rule Over Anything Else If You Can't Rule Over Yourself?

"Watch over your heart with all diligence,
for from it flow the springs of life."
~ Proverbs 4:23

Time for a quick review.

The place to start when it comes to finding your purpose is to realize God has made you in His image and has called you to play your part in His Dominion Mandate. This involves ruling over the domain He has entrusted to you, and doing it for His glory.

The domain He gives you may be large or small. This makes no difference. What counts is that you are faithful with what He has entrusted you to do.

The idea that God calls you to rule over a portion of the world is an exciting one. It gives life a purpose that's lasting and worthwhile. I cannot think of anything as rewarding as knowing you are doing what God has given you to do. Nor can I think of anything more motivating.

This is inspiring to think about. But there's a precondition for making it real for you. You have to rule yourself before you can be a true captain of the domain

God entrusted to your command.

Everybody wants to rule the world, but nobody wants to rule himself. But rule ourselves we must if we are to fulfill the purpose God has for us.

To bring God's rule to the world through your calling is a noble work. It makes life worth living. But this can't happen unless you get dominion over your own life.

Get Dominion or Be Dominated

When God created mankind and issued the Dominion Mandate, He designed us to be active, not passive. This is understandable, because filling the earth and subduing it requires activity.

Most people, unfortunately, are far more passive than active. They spend their lives waiting for events to happen in their favor, and then they respond. In the meantime they are led about by various impulses which are often destructive.

To understand this situation further, it's useful to recognize that everyone lives his or her life serving one of two masters. You are either a slave of sin or slave of righteousness.

The slave of sin believes he is his own master. He thinks because he's living the way he wants to live he's free. But the reality is he's blinded by his pride and enslaved to his sinful nature.

The slave of righteousness gladly admits he's not the master, but a servant. That's alright with him because he knows he's a servant of the One who has created the world. And he knows that as He serves Him he is free.

These two possibilities are the only options that exist. Slave of sin or slave of righteousness. There's no way to opt-out or negotiate a third way. It's the way God made the world.

Where you find yourself in this is at the foundation of living out your purpose. One way leads to futility and death, the other meaning and life.

Either get dominion or get dominated.

So as you think about your life, you either get dominion, or you get dominated. You either actively pursue the calling God gives you to bring dominion to your corner of the world, or you are dominated by your fallen nature inherited from Adam.

Your Identity
Whether you're actively bringing your life under the Lord's dominion depends in large part on your view of yourself, or your identity.

How do you see yourself? As a human animal at the furthest end of an evolutionary continuum? As a victim of all that has happened to you? As a no good rotten bum who has barely accomplished anything in life?

If any of these apply, you will be extremely limited when it comes to finding and living your purpose. Your future and your accomplishments will be confined by the resources you are able to find within yourself. To put it bluntly, you will miss the life you could be living.

The good news is there's a way to see your life differently and experience your full potential, and that's in receiving

149

a new identity.

In the first part of this book I explained three aspects of humanity. First, I explained that God created human beings to fill the earth and subdue it. Second, I showed how mankind has been corrupted by sin, and that this brought a huge disruption to God's original plan to bring dominion to the world. And third, I explained that through Christ's redemption the Dominion Mandate has been restored, and we've been commissioned to fulfill it.

Through Christ's redemption, all who entrust their lives to Him receive a new identity. They are no longer defined by their failings or limitations, but by who they are in Jesus Christ. This means that in Him you are able to see yourself as a restored individual. One who has been made whole and empowered to fulfill the mission God has for you.

One of the best parts of this new identity is that you are not limited to your own resources. As you live in union with Christ, you are able to experience all the grace, power, and wisdom He has for you. And it's through this relationship you become all that God has designed you to be.

It's in living with this identity you are able to rule your life according to God's principles, because through this identity you are no longer bound, but free. You are free from patterns of thinking and acting that hold you back and free to live out the fullness of your purpose in Christ.

Finding your freedom is a slippery business. The conventional wisdom claims you're free when you have complete control over your life. . . when you are the one calling the shots. But the unconventional truth is you are most free when you release your grip on the controls to the One who is really in charge. . . and live out the purpose He has for you.

Giving up control to gain freedom is hard to fathom, but it's reality. In submission to Christ our humanity is made new. And as part of the new humanity we become free to live as He made us.

Getting Over Your Past

A common obstacle for people trying to be free to fulfill their purpose is that they feel shackled by their past.

Everyone has a past. There's not a soul who has not sinned, acted foolishly, or been burdened with some regret. But just because you have failed somewhere in the past does not mean you have no future. God keeps giving you life, and it's for a reason.

I understand your past may haunt you. It does for many people. But God has made provision for you to move on with your life. You can be confident of this for the following reasons.

First, God forgives. Atonement for your failings does not come from beating yourself up or sabotaging your efforts to succeed. The atonement sufficient to cover your guilt comes by looking to Jesus Christ, the only perfect sacrifice for sin. Don't wallow in your shame, but have faith in Christ for forgiveness and peace.

Second, God is sovereign over your past. God knows everything about you—even the ways you've messed up. Because He knows all, He's in a position to use all for good. This includes the bad stuff. Did God not take the unjust murder of His Son and use it for good? He can do the same with the bad in your life.

Third, God has a future for you. Remember, He has a

track record of using people who have done foolish and even evil things. Prime examples are King David and the Apostle Paul. What's most important is not how flawless your record is, but how humble and obedient you are now. If your heart is sincerely turned to Him today, He will use you.

Yes, you have a past. So does everyone. Get over it, and get on with serving Him. You've learned some good lessons. Start applying them with the gifts He's provided you.

More About Getting Over Your Past

There is a bit more that needs to be said about the influence of your past on your life.

Regret over your failures is not the only way your past can hold you back. You can be kept from experiencing God's purpose if you dwell on what you believe was wrong about the circumstances of your past.

There is no shortage of people who believe life has dealt them a bad hand. These people will say things to themselves like:

> ➢ My parents didn't know what they were doing.

> ➢ We never had enough money.

> ➢ I never had good opportunities.

> ➢ I got a bad education.

> ➢ I missed out on my childhood.

> ➢ I've been abused.

> ➢ I've been scarred for life.

Those who say these kinds of things to themselves usually carry deep resentments. They think they've been cheated and are determined to pull themselves up by their own efforts and live the kind of life they really want to. But no matter how hard they try, they always seem to be stuck.

Doing what you can to overcome the deficiencies of your past is good. It's even admirable. But when the desire to overcome the past is driven by bitterness, it usually doesn't turn out well. Those motivated this way are in inner turmoil. They want to take their lives entirely into their own hands. They want to fix what they believe is amiss and prove their worth. But because the trouble going on inside is never resolved, they're in bondage and can't move ahead.

How do you become unstuck? I would sum it up in one word: REST.

> ➤ Rest in the knowledge that the sovereign Lord of the universe has overseen your whole life.

> ➤ Rest in the freedom the forgiveness of others brings you.

> ➤ Rest in the assurance that God can use every detail of your experience to make you the kind of person who can bring enormous value to the world.

> ➤ Rest in the love that God has shown you, and you can show others.

When you are able to rest you become free. But to rest and be truly free you must trust and believe.

> "You have made us for yourself, O Lord, and our hearts are restless until they rest in you."
>
> ~ St. Augustine

Emotional Maturity

Another area where people are often hindered in fulfilling their purpose is in the area of emotions. To make the most of your life in the Lord, the ability to manage your emotions is essential.

God made us emotional creatures. That's because He made us in His image, and He is an emotional being. Since God has emotions, we know that having emotions ourselves is not bad, but our emotions need to be managed.

The influence of The Fall on our emotional nature commonly pushes people toward one of two extremes.

One is denial. Men, especially, often deny they are affected by emotions, but their emotions influence them, just as women's do. Men are just more inclined to bottle them up. People who try and bottle up their emotions tend to be more reactive. They act like stoics most of the time, and then suddenly blow their cork.

The other extreme is excuse making. In this case people will blame their behavior on their emotions. They won't take responsibility for their actions, but resign themselves to being controlled by their feelings. And they'll use their out of control emotions to justify their behavior to others.

Both situations are common, and because of it, many are weighed down with emotional baggage. Those under this burden have a hard time focusing on the purpose God has for them. They are too caught up reacting to perceived slights and nursing old wounds to get the traction they need to move ahead with their lives.

A good way to get dominion over your emotions is to evaluate the story you are telling yourself. If you keep rehearsing thoughts that you've been cheated or treated unfairly, you will reinforce feelings of resentment, and you will become bitter. Bitter feelings have a way of enslaving you. If you do not get dominion over them, they will cause you to miss the purpose God has for you today.

How do you overcome destructive emotional patterns? Change the story you are telling yourself.

Instead of seeing yourself as a victim, see yourself as one who lives in this fallen world, but who, through faith in Christ, knows you are being redeemed by God's grace. Tell yourself that those around you are doing their best based on their understanding, and their nature, so there's no point being upset with them. Instead, keep telling yourself that God has called you to whatever He has called you to—and be busy with it.

> Growing in emotional maturity is really about becoming more oriented to the Lord and what He is doing, and less preoccupied with ourselves.

Growing in emotional maturity is really about becoming more oriented to the Lord and what He is doing, and less preoccupied with ourselves.

155

Much of the teaching about self-esteem in recent years has been misguided in that it leads us to put too much focus on ourselves. What we really need is to be more forgetful of ourselves and more mindful of the mission God has for each of us.

The Power of Habits

To rule yourself consistently, and in a way that allows you to effectively fulfill your calling, you have to pay attention to your habits.

There is a principle of sowing and reaping described in the Bible that can't be denied (Galatians 6:7, 8). You sow to the flesh and you reap corruption, but sow to the Spirit and reap life.

This is one of those undeniable truths. So pay attention to the habits that shape your life.

Improving one's habits follows a principle of replacement. In other words, you improve them by putting off the old habit you need to get rid of and putting on the new habit that will do you good (Ephesians 4:22ff.).

I encourage you to examine your own practices. Here is a quick survey of habits to get you started as you consider your own patterns. The negative habits will hold you back from answering your calling as you should. The positive ones will serve to move you ahead.

NEGATIVE HABITS
Time Wasters. There are many time wasting habits that keep people from achieving the purpose God has for them. Television watching used to be the biggest time waster, but I think it's been replaced by online diversions. Today, it's checking Facebook and email that people do to avoid

their work. Sure, these tools can help you stay in touch, but they can also waste a lot of time you could spend more productively.

Addictions. Some of the time wasters just mentioned are addictive, but here I'm thinking of more destructive behaviors like addictions to alcohol, drugs, and pornography. These addictions often arise because the emotional issues mentioned in the previous section have never been resolved. The good news is that sometimes just getting clear on one's purpose in life is enough to break the bonds of an addiction. The bad news is that there are many who would rather ruin their lives than embrace their true purpose and change.

Bitterness. It's not normally thought of this way, but bitterness is a habit. It's made a habit by rehearsing over and over again the offenses—real and imagined—that have been committed against you. Bitterness can become a root that's hard to extract, but get it out you must if you want to fulfill your purpose in life. There is only one way to get rid of bitterness. It's called forgiveness.

Covetousness. What is covetousness? Covetousness is desiring the fruit produced by another person following his calling while neglecting the attention you should be giving your own calling. The antidote to covetousness is contentment—both with your calling, and the fruit your calling produces.

POSITIVE HABITS
Drawing near to God. Positive change does not come about from our own efforts alone. It is dependent on the grace of God. This gives us good reason to make regular use of the means God gives us to know Jesus and grow in Him. These include worship, prayer, Bible reading, the Lord's Supper, and the fellowship of God's people. To

157

neglect these means is to disregard the primary way God has given for you to experience change.

Gratitude. Gratitude has a way of opening your eyes. It helps you see that all you have comes from above. Gratitude also seems to open God's hand to release further blessings your way. I know of some people who have started a "Gratitude Journal" to help them become more thankful. This is a good way to make gratitude a habit. Keep in mind gratitude should always be a sincere expression of thanks, and never manipulative.

Practice virtues. We know we need to practice to gain athletic skill or musical proficiency, but how about practicing virtue? Practicing virtues like purity, self-control, generosity, diligence, patience, kindness, and humility can go a long way to make you more proficient in your calling.

Courage. I like what the original 1828 Webster's Dictionary has to say about courage. It speaks of courage as being that which enables a man to face danger or difficulties in a way that's firm, resolute, and bold, without fear or depression of spirits. This is good, because it's exactly what you need if you're going to persistently pursue your purpose in life. Make a habit of showing courage.

There are many other habits to consider, but this is a start.

We all have habits, yet few pay attention to the significant place their specific habits have in shaping their lives.

Habits are like strong cords. They can either pull you forward or pull you back. Your habits can make or break you, so take great care over the habits you develop.

I've always admired those who are able to make what they do look easy. It doesn't matter if it's an athlete, musician, public speaker, or whatever. If the one doing it makes it look as simple as ABC, I'm impressed.

The truth, of course, is that which looks easy rarely is. Sure, certain people have gifts that allow them to perform certain tasks more naturally. But we all know of highly gifted people who have squandered their natural advantages. And, for those who are diligent, it takes hours and hours to fully develop what they've got.

That's why I'm impressed, because those who are able to make it look easy have more than gifts. They have the ability to rule themselves. And that's something the rest of us need, no matter what we're called to do.

The Art of Self-Government

It's hard to overemphasize the place that ruling yourself well has in achieving your life's purpose. If you rule over yourself poorly, you can't advance. You'll be stuck. **But if you rule yourself diligently, you will be prepared to rule an expanding domain.**

Think of yourself as a governor. As governor, you are responsible to rule yourself effectively. The better you rule yourself, the more you can be used by God. And the more likely He will place you in positions of greater influence for His kingdom.

You may never find yourself ruling over organizations that involve multiple people as in a church, business organization, or the civil government. But you can be sure when you practice the art of self-government well, it will benefit your realm no matter what your area of activity— or how big that realm may be. This applies even if it's just within your own family.

Constantly seek the grace of God to help you rule yourself faithfully. As you do, God will open up a whole new world for you.

Summary

◆ To advance God's dominion through your calling you need to first get dominion over your own life.

◆ Getting dominion over your life requires you to live as a slave of righteousness rather than a slave of sin.

◆ The freedom necessary to rule your life well comes as you trust God and submit to His Word.

◆ God has a future for those with a past.

◆ Managing your emotions is an important part of getting dominion over your life. Getting control of your emotions often has to do with changing the story you are telling yourself.

◆ Your ability to rule yourself consistently is greatly influenced by your habits, both positive and negative.

◆ You'll be in a better position to be used by God when you can manage your life well.

Make it Personal

1. What is it that seeks to dominate you, and keep your from managing your life as you desire?

2. What emotional issues do you need to resolve to better rule over your life?

3. What negative habits do you need to put off and what positive habits do you need to put on?

Chapter 12

Keep the Vision

How to Stay Focused
in the Right Direction

"He who began a good work in you
will bring it to completion. . ."
~ Philippians 1:6 (ESV)

I began this book quoting the verse from the book of Proverbs that tells us without a vision people perish (Pr. 29:18). I mentioned the verse there because a major problem people have is they don't have a vision of why they are here. In this chapter I'd like to elaborate on the concept of vision.

Most people get the basic idea of vision. They understand that to have vision is to have a focused mental picture of where you need to be headed in life. With this in mind, the proverb makes sense. If you don't have a vision or an idea where you need to be going, you are lost.

This seems clear enough. **What people struggle with is how to get vision—and keep it once you've got it.**

For most, vision is a mystery. To them, there's no good explanation why some have a clear picture of where they need to go while others have no picture at all. It seems like you have vision or you don't, and if you don't, there's nothing you can do about it.

Well, there's good news. This whole vision thing is not as mysterious as you may think. Living with vision is well within reach, but first, you need to understand what the proverb actually means by "vision."

When this proverb uses the word vision, it's not referring to a mystical direction that you or some leader may have received in an inexplicable way. It's talking about what God has revealed in His Word. We know this because the parallel part of the same verse uses the word "law" instead of vision.

This is good news because it means the vision God has for your life is accessible to you. It's in His Word. And it's as you learn His Word and apply it to your circumstances you are able to live with the vision you need to fulfill the purpose God has for you.

Following a Bible-derived vision is what you need to move ahead with the direction God has for you. But it's not all you need. You also need to maintain the vision to keep going the way the Lord leads you.

Stumbling Blocks

There's a sense of excitement that goes along with knowing what God wants you to do with your life. But knowing and executing are two different things. So be prepared, implementing your vision may take some time.

Because implementation might be prolonged, you must maintain your vision if you're going to be faithful to it. This can be a challenge. There are various forces at work that can make it difficult for you to keep your vision from slipping away.

Here are the most common issues that can cause you to lose your vision. Being aware of them can make you better prepared to overcome them when they arise.

Fear

The Bible warns us about fear many times. Jesus repeatedly urged his followers to "fear not." These warnings still apply, and you need to heed them if you are going to pursue the course God has prepared for you.

Fear can cripple you. It can blind you from seeing reality accurately and can bind you from doing what you know ought to be done. So learn how to deal with the fears that stand in the way of doing what God wants you to do.

Most fears are way overblown. Usually, what we fear never comes about. And even if it does, it's not as bad as we imagined it.

So how do you overcome the fear that can hold you back? By faith, hope, and love. Have faith in God who is leading you. Put your hope in His promises. And allow love to drive out your fears so that pleasing God and serving others come before yourself. This will help keep fear at bay—and your vision intact.

Concerns About Security

The desire for security is understandable—especially in a world filled with risks and uncertainty. Finding a reasonable level of security is not just prudent, it's responsible.

But concerns over security can be overdone. When you're too preoccupied with your security, it can keep you from making the life changes and progress that's within your reach.

Risk is an unavoidable part of finding your purpose. If

you don't take risks, you will become stagnant which makes you vulnerable in a different way. It's far better to keep moving ahead in faith, finding your security in the Lord.

The Old Testament tells us of a time when God's people craved the security of Egypt more than the blessings of the Promised Land (Ex.16:3). Ever since, it's been the norm for people to prefer the comfort of what's known—even if the situation stinks—over the uneasiness caused by uncertainty.

Excessive concern about security is not difficult to overcome. Here's the secret: it's in realizing your greatest security comes not from preserving your own place, but following what God is laying before you.

The safest place for any of us is in the center of God's will, no matter how challenging that place may be.

Hardship

If you're like most, you'd much rather have smooth sailing than rough waters. After all, who wants to expend energy and endure suffering if you don't have to?

This tendency leads people to seek to avoid hardship at all costs. Avoiding hardship sounds sensible—until you realize practically any progress in life involves some hardship.

Don't let hardship keep you from pursuing the vision God has given you. Hardship is part of life in a fallen world. No great accomplishment has been achieved by anyone without some adversity. And as you endure hardship, it will make you stronger.

Remember this when you face obstacles in pursuit of your calling. When difficulties come your way, it will be easy to question what you are doing. You may wonder, "Am I on the right track? If I am, why is it so hard?"

Whether something is easy or difficult is an unreliable gauge when it comes to deciding if you ought to do it or not. If every difficulty were taken as a sign to give up, not much of value would get done.

When difficulties do come—and they will—you will find strength to persevere by going back and rehearsing your calling. Reflect on what God has shown you. Review your purpose, and submit yourself to the Lord anew. This is likely all you'll need to forge ahead in the direction God has shown you.

Faulty Standards of Success
Here's an irony to be aware of as you pursue your vision. You may actually feel like a failure when you are successfully following the purpose God has for you.

That sounds strange, but it happens all the time when people have the wrong standard of success.

I mentioned earlier the world measures success by money, power, and visible influence. But if you are doing what you believe God wants you to, you may not look very successful by these indicators.

Don't let this deceive you or discourage you. Just because you may be laboring in obscurity, without the kind of external rewards you might like, does not mean you are failing. You need to think longer term, and remember that obedience brings its own rewards in due time.

Other People's Opinions
If you are the kind of person who is sensitive to what God's Spirit is doing in your heart, there is a good chance

you're also sensitive to the opinions of others. The former you want to cultivate. The latter you want to filter carefully.

As you pursue your calling, remain responsive to the Lord. This will help you stay on track and position you for blessings to come. But don't feel like you have to be responsive to everyone with an opinion about your life. Otherwise, you'll have a hard time not being swayed from your path.

There is a difference between getting advice from others and taking their opinions as gospel.

Getting advice is good. So surround yourself with wise counselors, but be careful of other's opinions—especially unsolicited opinions—as they can throw you into a state of self-doubt. In the end, you have to do your own thinking—and believing.

As I've talked with others about the significant breakthroughs they've had in their lives, there seems to be a common thread: they came to a point where they cared less about what others thought and more about what they believed they were called to accomplish.

Remember, the One who has given you a mandate to fulfill is God; not those who have little real knowledge of what your life is about. Keep in tune with the purpose God has for you, and don't let the purposes others may have for you get in the way.

168

These are all obstacles you need to be aware of. I've spent some time with them because they are so common and can easily derail you. By recognizing them and knowing how to respond, you can put them in their proper place and keep yourself on course.

Besides being prepared for these obstacles, there are also some positive, pro-active steps to help you remain undeterred in pursuing the vision God has given you.

Work at developing yourself as a person, especially spiritually. How well you progress with your purpose will rise and fall with your development as a human being.

Also, strive to maintain coherence between what you seek to accomplish with your life and who you are on the inside. True success flows out of your inner being, or who you are as a person. It doesn't come from playing a part like an actor.

To help you develop yourself as a person, maintain your vision, and live in keeping with your calling, here are several activities worth practicing regularly.

Worship God faithfully. Come into God's presence for worship on a weekly basis. Worship is not only the Lord's way to help you keep your focus; it is how He renews you in Christ's likeness, and further equips you to serve Him and live out your part in the Dominion Mandate. Regular worship in a faithful church is the most important thing you can do to live in keeping with the purpose God has for you.

Read good books. Reading good books is time well spent. I define a good book as one that lifts you to a new level of understanding. A good book is like a good friend who brings new ways of looking at your circumstances.

169

Especially look for books that will further equip you to advance your purpose. And, of course, God's Word should be on the top of anyone's list.

Spend time with quality companions. Choose wisely whom you spend time with. The companion of fools suffers harm (Pr.13:20). Interacting with people who are wiser and more experienced than you will challenge and lift you up. "As iron sharpens iron so one man sharpens another" (Pr. 27:17). Don't spend time with the same group of people just because you're comfortable with them.

Watch your thought life. Most of what you encounter in life you cannot control, but you can control your thoughts. Do not let negative, destructive thoughts camp out in your mind. They will put you in a hole quicker than you know and tempt you to question your whole life's direction. Think on those things that are true, honorable, right, pure, etc... (Phil 4:8).

Use your imagination constructively. Learn to use your imagination in a way that leads to you do good. God cursed the world when every imagination of man's heart was only evil continually, but when man uses his imagination in a God-honoring way, it becomes a means of blessing. Make it a practice to prayerfully envision what God can do through you as you submit yourself to Him.

Keep your life in perspective. Remember, it's not all about you and what is happening in your life. It is more about God and what He's doing in the world. This perspective releases the pressure and allows you to focus on how to best serve with your life. It also helps you accept your short comings, and even laugh at them now and then, while still taking your life seriously.

Fulfilling your mission in the world is a long-term project.

It is not a sprint, but a marathon. There will be times when you "hit the wall." But when God gives a calling, He supplies grace to finish the race. Your task is to keep your focus on the prize, and keep running.

Summary

◆ Acquiring a vision is accessible to all. It comes not by mystical experience but by applying God's Word to your situation.

◆ These common issues cause vision to be lost: fear, concerns about security, hardship, faulty standards of success, and other peoples' opinions.

◆ Your progress in implementing your vision will rise and fall with your overall development as a person.

◆ You'll be helped in your personal development and maintenance of your vision as you: worship God faithfully, read good books, find quality companions, watch your thought life, use your imagination constructively, and keep your life in perspective.

Make it Personal

1. What is your vision for your life?

2. What hinders you from implementing your vision?

3. What do you believe is the biggest step you need to take to follow your vision?

Chapter 13

Choose This Day

You Will Never Experience Your Purpose Without Taking Action

"How long will you hesitate between two opinions?
If the Lord is God, follow Him. . ."
~ 1 Kings 18:21

To spend your life making God's rule known through your calling may be a completely new idea to you. This isn't surprising in light of the smorgasbord of philosophies existing today.

Views of God's relation to the world vary. Some—although still a tiny, but growing, percentage—see God as non-existent. Others believe He may have set the world in motion, but now leaves it for us to figure out how to live in it. Then, there are those who see God actively bringing comfort and guidance to His people, but without a plan to advance the blessings of His kingdom through history.

Scripture reveals God to have something different in mind. The Bible reveals God's plan to redeem the world, and use those who trust Him to usher in this transformation. This is not only possible, but certain to occur. That's because Jesus Christ came as a new Adam to restore all, and bring all, into submission to Him.

Once you realize what God is doing in the world, and

understand His purpose for you in it, it's possible to live a life that is rich with meaning. But it takes more than getting your thinking straight to fulfill your purpose. You have to choose to actually live in keeping with what you understand. You have to take action.

Take Action

When you understand that God has a purpose for your activities in this world, it opens up a whole new way of thinking. You are able to see life is about more than just survival, or filling your days to keep busy or entertained. It's about using the days you have to advance God's kingdom as much as possible.

> It takes more than getting your thinking straight to fulfill your purpose.

This has the potential to bring meaning and focus to every minute of your day. Wouldn't you like to live this way? You can, but you have to make a choice. Will you live your life for the Kingdom of God or the kingdom of mammon? Remember, you're devoting yourself to one or the other. Once you choose, you need to take action. Nothing happens without action.

You can think, wait for the right time, or pray, but until you act in the direction God is showing you, nothing will be any different.

Unfortunately, too many people are immobilized and never act on what they know. Fear, doubts, and negativity hold them back. So nothing is any different for them. And they never experience the thrill of moving toward what could be.

But I hope it is different for you. Please, take action.

174

You don't need to have your whole future mapped out in order to take the first step. It's impossible to accurately forecast your future anyway; because once you start all you see around you will look different. This is good, because the differences you see will provide the feedback you need to take the next step.

There's a verse in the book of Proverbs that says, "Commit your works to the Lord, and your plans will be established" (Pr.16:3). I've heard plenty of people assume this verse means that if you just make plans, and commit them to the Lord in prayer, He will see to it they succeed.

This interpretation has always bothered me. For one, the verse says we are to commit our works to the Lord, not our plans. Also, to assume God will just rubber stamp our plans into reality seems terribly presumptuous.

So, what does this verse mean?

I believe it means this. . .

In whatever works you believe you ought to do, do them unto the Lord. As you do, He will lead you, and unfold your plans as you go forward.

A Higher Purpose

If you have difficulty acting on what you know God wants you to do, you always need to come back to this: God has a higher purpose for your life.

If you're stuck with a vision no bigger than putting in your 70 plus years and deciding what you're looking forward to on T.V. this week, it's going to be hard to come up with the 'get up and go' to tackle anything substantial.

But if you know you're called by God to do something specific with your life, you better get busy. I'm a believer there should be urgency to life. You have something to accomplish, and the clock is running down. There's no time to waste.

I suspect if you've read this far, you want to be among the doers. You don't want to waste your life, but want to play your part in God's grand plan for humanity. That's good. Keep nurturing your aspirations, but be sure there is movement in the direction you need to be going.

One way to help you get moving is to see yourself as a cause as opposed to an effect.

Most people see themselves as an effect. They're conditioned to be primarily passive, and they live in a responsive mode. They are compliant in a way that's not constructive, and as a consequence, their lives are shaped by all the cultural forces and demands pressing upon them.

But God created you to be a causative agent. He made you so you would take action, with the expectation your actions would lead to certain effects in the real world.

In creating you this way, God clearly has more in mind than just having you "think" about living according to His purpose. He wants you to be consumed with His purpose, and have it drive all your activity.

He wants you to take dominion.

This only happens when you treasure what He values more than what the world values, and you have a sense of urgency about your calling that gets you moving.

Such a Time as This

We live in cynical and pessimistic times. People are so hypnotized by bad news they see little point in taking action. Many have resigned themselves to live with a sense of impending doom, and are just waiting for calamity to befall them.

I can sympathize with this outlook. There are plenty of signs of decadence today. And much corruption, too. And if all I did was soak myself in the news of the latest zombie attack or government power grab, any thought about doing good to bring about constructive change would seem fruitless.

But there is another way of looking at our situation. You can see it as an opportunity.

When a culture is falling apart, it reveals the status quo is not working. Further, it reveals that self-worship in a society leads to ruin.

> When a culture is dying, it presents the opportunity to replace it with something better.

This situation presents an opportunity to replace corrupt and decadent systems with one that brings the life of God to people. By paying attention and taking action, you can be among those who bring about needed change.

And this is precisely what we should be doing.

Instead of being scared and paralyzed by fear, consider what you can do. Take into account all you have learned, and the experiences you've had, and how God may have placed you where you are now for such a time as this.

Our times cry out for God-honoring game changers. And that's exactly what God is calling you to be right now, by getting dominion in your own life and the domain He has given you.

A Greater Glory
Sometimes people are hesitant to take the action they need to because they are caught up in desiring the wrong kind of glory.

God has placed within us a desire for glory, so it's right to want to experience it. But with the Fall, this desire was perverted. Now, by default, we seek our own glory, and everybody wants to be a rock star.

The pursuit of self-glory leads to pain and misery, both for us and others. And, it takes us from our true purpose. We were not made to seek our own glory, but the glory of God who created us. As we partake of His glory we experience a glory far better than the glory men strive to achieve in this world. It's an incomparable glory that endures through eternity.

How do we partake of His glory?

It starts with denying ourselves, and willingly sacrificing our own interests for the interests of others. This is known as "the way of the cross," and it's indispensable when it comes to sharing in the glory of God.

We partake of His glory as we pursue our everyday callings with character. The glory of God does not come outside our ordinary labors, but through them. So, whatever you do, do it in keeping with God's standards. It doesn't matter if you're a mother, customer service rep, doctor, or driver of a recycling truck.

Have the goal of "His glory" before you at all times. Go after it aggressively. Strive to see His kingdom advance through your prayers and service.

"Whether you eat or drink or whatever you do, do all to the glory of God" (1 Corinthians 10:31).

The surest way to trip yourself up regarding God's purpose for your life is to be obsessed with your own glory. But when you willingly give up your glory for His, you receive your part in a greater glory.

> "Not to us, O LORD, not to us, but to Your name give glory, because of your lovingkindness, because of Your truth." ~Joshua 24:35

Goals

Any book on developing yourself and fulfilling your purpose would be incomplete without a section on goals. So, here goes.

My own thought about goals is they need to be approached flexibly and with realistic expectations.

Goals are not the powerful force they are sometimes made out to be. According to some authors, if you are diligent to set your goals and work at them, you will get all you want out of life. That might be true if we had absolute sovereignty over our lives, but we don't. No matter how good you become at ruling your domain, God's rule is still supreme, and He may choose to mess with your plans.

Also, even when goals are diligently pursued, they may not be met for other reasons. Intangible issues like feelings of guilt or a lack of confidence often hold people back from the prize they seek. The good news is that being aware of these barriers can sometimes lead to just the personal breakthrough that's needed.

To be clear, I'm all for setting goals. In most cases, well-defined goals are exactly what it takes to keep us on track and help us to accomplish what's possible. This book, for example, would never have been completed without a series of goals.

Taking all this into account, here's a suggested approach to goal setting.

First, make a habit of regularly setting goals for all areas of your life. But be willing to modify them as you grow and your life changes. If it becomes obvious your goals need altering, revise them.

Second, ask yourself some basic questions to guide you as you form your goals. Here are a few suggested questions.

What do you want to accomplish? Think long-term first. From the perspective of your death bed, consider what you want to achieve in your life. Then, determine what must happen to accomplish what you envision. Setting targets one, two, five, ten, and twenty years out can help bring order to the tasks needed to accomplish your goals.

How are you going to get there? You need to find the

means to the end. Will accomplishing your goals require further training, relocating your family, or changing your line of work? Don't be afraid to face these kinds of questions. You must if you want to be realistic about moving ahead.

What's the next step? To start making progress, it's essential to identify the next step. If you don't, you'll never start. Your next step may be simply to gather more information. Whatever it is, make sure it is clearly defined. Then follow through. Do it, and plan additional steps.

In all your goal-setting, do not lose sight of the larger objective, which is to fulfill the purpose God has for you by maximizing all He has given you.

Rise Up to God's Definition of Who You Are

Choosing a new course of action for your life can seem overwhelming, especially if you're emotionally tied to the values and expectations of those who surround you. Even if you try to venture outside the expectations of others, an emotional tether might keep you from venturing very far before snapping you back.

This is why it can be extremely hard to lead yourself and others in a new direction. But it is possible, if you insist on being defined by God alone, thinking His thoughts after Him.

Think about it. How has anyone ever accomplished anything great in God's name? By living with the knowledge that God's assessment is more important than any man's.

Most people allow others to define them. Sometimes this is because others will try to control the people who are close to them for their own reasons. Other times people assume what those around them expect, and fall in line.

When you allow others to define you, you can't be free to pursue God's vision for your life. The plans others have will always loom over you. This doesn't lead to a very happy or fulfilling existence. It keeps you from being faithful to God, too.

Rise up to God's definition of who you are. He made you, sustains you, and put His claim on your life. Nobody else has a right to define you as a person. You are obligated to show honor where honor is due, but the only way you should allow yourself to be defined is by your relationship with God.

You are made in His image. You've been called to fulfill His purpose for you in the world. And it's on this basis you can go forth using the gifts and fulfilling the opportunities He's given you with confidence.

As you get the first inkling of the direction God would have you go, choose to take action. There's nothing to be gained if you delay.

"Choose this day whom you will serve."
~Joshua 24:35

Summary

◆ Living out your purpose calls for more than getting your thinking straight. You need to act on what you understand.

◆ You do not need your whole future planned to take action. You only need to take the next step.

◆ Remembering that God has a higher purpose for your life should help propel you forward.

◆ Beware of pessimism. Too many are immobilized by bad news. Consider what you can do in the place God has you.

◆ God created us with a desire for glory. We partake of His glory as we deny ourselves and follow His calling on our lives.

◆ Set goals to keep yourself on track, but be flexible enough to modify them if life changes warrant it.

◆ The way to overcome the expectations of others and choose the course God has laid before you is to always rise up to His definition of who you are.

Make it Personal

1. What do you believe God may be putting before you to do?

2. What "next step" should you take?

3. How does letting God define who you are help you take the action necessary to fulfill your life's purpose?

Chapter 14

Dominion By Grace

From Start to Finish, God Has Provided the Way to Be Fully Human

"For from Him and through Him and to Him are all things.
To Him be the glory forever. Amen."
~ Romans 11:36

The journey of God's people to the Promised Land is among the most familiar accounts in the Bible. It's found in the book of Numbers, and is rich in instruction for those who want to fulfill God's purpose for their lives.

When God delivered His people from the slavery and oppression of Egypt, He did so to deliver them to a much better land. A place known as the Promised Land. A land like no other, filled with milk and honey.

All God's people had to do to enter this land was to faithfully follow Him. God already made the provision, they just needed to hang on and do what He said. But they didn't. They doubted and complained, and lacked the courage to enter the land prepared for them. All they could think of were the giants in the land, and this scared them away.

Because of unbelief, this generation never did enter the Promised Land. They craved the security of Egypt and wandered in the wilderness for 40 years. That's right, 40 years. Eventually, the entire generation died off, except for a believing few who led the descendants of the fallen into the new land.

Sadly, the first generation forfeited their purpose.

Entering Your Promised Land

The record we have of Israel's failure to take the Promised Land is more than just an account from that nation's history. It's a model for all who come after that generation.

Today, the land God has for us is not merely a limited section of the Middle East. It covers the earth. When Jesus Christ gave the Great Commission to disciple all nations, He was in effect telling us that the new Promised Land is the whole world. Now go and win it.

> There is a promised land that remains.

As we pursue this renewed mandate, we must remember the lessons of the original Promised Land experience. These lessons can be summed up simply: quit complaining and show some courage as you go after the blessings God has in store for you.

Soon after the deliverance from Egypt, the people started complaining. They saw no way they could survive the path they were on, and they missed Egypt's food. They should have showed courage and pressed into the land waiting for them. Because they didn't, they missed out.

These lessons should not be lost to us. Those who

succeed in fulfilling what God has for them are not complainers. They're people with courage, and they're doers. Remember this. If you want to experience God's calling, you can't grumble about the difficulty you find along the way. Be strong and courageous.

There is a promised land that remains, and God's promise of blessing to those who trust Him still holds true. But you must boldly go after the blessing in order to find it.

Here's a message for anyone who has been made complacent by their misunderstanding of grace:

Grace does not give you the license to do nothing. Grace gives you the ability to do what God has prepared for you.

It's All By Grace

In this book you've probably noticed a certain emphasis on what you need to be doing. I've told you that to fulfill your part of the Dominion Mandate you need to find your calling, live with integrity, embrace work, endure hardship, keep the vision, and so on. It involves a lot of doing.

There are some faithful believers who may object to this. They might argue that all this talk of what we need to do is contrary to the Bible's message of grace.

But there's no need to come to that conclusion. When grace gives us faith that is alive, it leads to action, and it produces good works. In fact, "faith, if it has no works, is dead" (James 2:17).

The good works the Bible expects of us are not limited to works of charity. They include the works that occupy us in our everyday vocations. This means what we do in our work is a significant expression of God's grace in our lives.

If you drove through the countryside and came upon acres and acres of cultivated farmland, lined with row after row of well cared for vegetation, it would be reasonable to say the farmer who owned the land was blessed. But the fact is, you probably wouldn't think that, if all you did was drive by an empty field. That's because it took the efforts of the farmer to bring his blessing to its fullest realization.

This is in keeping with God's design, and it's in no way contrary to grace.

When God issued the Dominion Mandate, He told the first man to cultivate The Garden and keep it. This involved work. Where did the ability to do that work come from? It came from God's grace. Well, the ability to do our work comes from God's grace too. Since the Fall, the Dominion Mandate has remained in force, and so has the provision of His grace to fulfill it.

The greatest provision of God's grace has come through Jesus Christ. He was sent so all who believe in Him would experience the renewal necessary to fulfill God's original design. This experience is commonly regarded as "salvation," but it includes far more than waiting to die and go to heaven. It involves faithfully fulfilling the purpose God has for you as long as He gives you breath.

The Bible itself says, "By grace you have been saved through faith, and that not of yourself, it is the gift of God. Not as a result of works, so that no man should boast.

For you are His workmanship, created in Christ Jesus for good works, which God prepared beforehand that you would walk in them" (Ephesians 2:8-10).

God saves souls. In saving them, He has prepared ahead of time the good works they would perform in this life. To accomplish these works, His ongoing grace is required. From this, we can see that the full experience of God's purpose for your life is dependent on your spiritual growth in God's grace.

Jesus Christ entered the world as the ideal man. As we live in union with Him, we become as close to the ideal dominion man or woman possible, this side of heaven. And it's in this we find our greatest personal fulfillment and highest level of productivity for His kingdom.

Worship and the Church
Since there's a relationship between your spiritual growth and the fulfillment of your calling, developing yourself spiritually must be a priority. The way to maximize your spiritual development is through the church.

Despite the resistance to organized religion, the church remains God's training ground for His people. And as a body of people, the church is the salt of the earth and the light of the world. It is the leaven that permeates the world and brings the Kingdom of God to the earth.

This means the church is more than a gathered community on Sunday mornings. But it is no less than that either, and those who desire the weekly renewal God provides through worship will make a point to gather with the people of God.

Worship is at the heart of the Dominion Mandate.

We are used to referring to man as *homo sapiens,* or man the thinker.   More accurately, man should be described as *homo adorans,* man the worshiper.

God made man to worship.   As one who worships, he orients himself around an ultimate reference point. That point of reference can either be God or oneself.

When a man makes himself the reference point of his life, he becomes the center of all he does.   But God didn't make us to live at the center, because it leads to futility and death. When you live with God as the reference point of your life, from Him flows love in the service of others. Service that has as its purpose the advance of Christ's dominion.

Who is at the center of your life?   This question is fundamental to discovering and living your purpose. Even more basic, it's fundamental to living as a human being.

How to Live as a Human Being
As human beings we have many desires. Among the most important of these are desires for love and meaning and connectedness with others. Without these basics in your life, you are what an old work associate of mine used to call "one hurtin' puppy."

When a person is short on love or meaning, or detached from others, it ends up driving his behavior. He may deal with it by trying to prove himself or escaping through booze, drugs, sex, a hobby or career.   Some will isolate themselves in a state of inferiority, fear or anxiety. While others puff themselves up with pride and superiority. Some deny the existence of God.

All of these are coping mechanisms. None of them fills the heart to meet its need. Those who remain in this position end up hardened, and feel their humanity slipping away. This helps explain why we see so many hollow expressions and uncaring attitudes today. The number of people who live this way can't be counted, but no doubt the number is huge. How sad.

It's into this scenario God sent His Son to bring meaning, love and connectedness. Through His life, death, and resurrection, Jesus came that we would know the love of the Father and be restored to the purpose He has for us. To experience this love and the meaning only He gives, we only need to trust Him. That's all you need to fill the void. And from there it's about discovering the life God has for you.

It's through Jesus Christ that our humanity is recovered. Without Him, we're just cogs in the machinery of the universe. All we do is exist and seek to survive. Our chief interest becomes security punctuated by pleasure. And the type of pleasure we indulge only serves to harden us further. But through faith in Christ, we become a part of a new humanity. A humanity that is alive to love and do good. And actively bring Christ's dominion to the world.

This is a great work of transformation, and God does it all by His grace. He's the one who makes us, re-creates us, and gives us a mission to fulfill. And He's the one who will bring it all to a glorious consummation.

The ability of the gospel to renew our humanity is perhaps the most powerful testimony of its truth.

Gratitude

Sometimes as I talk to people about these concepts they show concern as to whether or not they really "get it." They think they understand what it all means, and they want to be hopeful that their lives can be different. But they also want to make sure they get it.

As I've observed these people, I can usually tell whether they get it or not. Those who do are happier, more patient, focused, and so on. But what particularly stands out is they are grateful. They are grateful for what God has done, and revealed to them. They are grateful to know their purpose—and it shows.

So, here's a point to remember. When you get what it means to be part of God's new humanity, you will be grateful. Grateful God has opened your eyes to the glorious plan He has for the world, and grateful He has given you a place to serve. So grateful you will want to do what He has ordained for you to do.

Summary

♦ Israel's failure to enter the Promised Land due to unbelief serves as a warning to every generation since. The major lesson to be learned: quit complaining and show courage as you go after the blessing God has for you.

♦ The call upon us to take action and do what God wants us to do does not contradict the Bible's message of grace.

♦ The church is God's training ground for spiritual growth, and those who desire to develop spiritually will not forsake her.

◆ God made man primarily as a worshipper. When man worships God, he is able to receive God's love and serve others.

◆ It's in receiving the grace of God and living out the Dominion Mandate to bring His transforming love to the world that we are made complete as human beings.

◆ A strong indicator that you understand and embrace the concepts of this book is gratitude.

Make it Personal

1. What "promised land" would God have you pursue?

2. What is the role of the church in your life, and what does it need to be?

3. In what way would pursuing the Dominion Mandate make you live more fully as a human being?

Conclusion

"The conclusion, when all has been heard, is:
fear God and keep His commandments,
because this applies to every person."
~ Ecclesiastes 12:13

Today's Scenario

Our society seems to be spinning out of control at an accelerating pace—economically, politically, socially, and spiritually. This puts a lot of pressure on individuals, like you and me, every day. Not only is there concern about the future, but questions about where we fit in. More people are wondering about their purpose, and whether their efforts make any difference.

The temptation is to give in to fear, and stand by idly as we wait for a catastrophe from which we cannot recover. But this is not a time for passivity. What we need to do is reclaim the Bible's first principles, and apply them to our generation. By first principles I'm referring specifically to the biblical truths that God created us in His image to take dominion over the world, and bring His rule to the world by applying His Word to all of life as we serve others.

Reality

An immediate benefit of recovering these first principles is it brings a needed understanding of reality. We live in a fallen world, where there is corruption, evil, heartache and loss. This reality makes us susceptible to a sense of futility, but it's not the whole story. Into this sin-scarred world, God sent His Son to bring redemption and restoration. Thanks to this gift, we can find our meaning and purpose, which is linked to the Dominion Mandate.

Each of us has been authorized by God to extend His kingdom. To equip us for this task, He gives us gifts and callings to use in our particular places and times. As we faithfully use what God has provided, we further His purpose and find our fulfillment. And it's through our faithfulness that we are used by God to bless to others.

Your Life

Life passes quickly. If you are in your 40s, as I am, you are already in the second half. Seniors tell me the clock runs faster during the second half than the first. I make this point because you need to decide what you are going to do with your life, now. The ideas in this book are not academic. They're practical, and have eternal consequences. They focus on where you are going in your life, and how to live each day.

My sense is that most people are waiting for someone to hand them the kind of life they want. I don't mean people are unwilling to work. Many are. But I do mean that most people don't want to do the kind of thinking and take the responsible action necessary to live the life God has for them. As a consequence, their creativity remains trapped and they never experience the connectedness they desire as human beings.

I urge you to be different. Be among those who are not afraid to look at reality as it is, and answer the call God has on your life. You have a unique contribution to offer the world, and the only way to live without regret is to deliver it. Your days are numbered. You can't control that. Yet you can control whether your life ends with, or without, regret. But you have to make a choice.

196

Love

The prime motive for devoting yourself to God's call on your life and ruling your little piece of the world for Him is love. This may surprise you, but love is the only force powerful enough to sustain you for a lifetime of service. It's also what you need to overcome any obstacles to fulfilling your life's mission.

Out of love, God made the world and is redeeming it through Jesus Christ. In response to this love, we are compelled to pursue His purpose for our lives gladly, with love. Love delivers you from fear, and strengthens you to venture into the unknown with faith. Love is what brings success.

Love leads to service. And the amount of love you have in your heart can be measured by the extent you are using your gifts and opportunities for the sake of the Dominion Mandate.

Get Dominion

Over fifteen years ago a friend of mine said good-bye to me with words that have stuck with me. He said to me, "Get dominion." I like those parting words better than any I've heard before. They carry with them an authority and optimism like no other.

As I bring this book to a close, I want to leave you with the same words.

Get dominion.

God has commissioned you to use all that He has given you to play your part in ruling over the world and developing it for His glory. As you are faithful to answer His call, you can be assured He will use your efforts to further His purpose in the world. This is true no matter how small your role may seem.

God is writing a glorious story through all of history. He intends for you to be a part of the story. Come join the action. There's a place for you.

Appendix A

The Way of Restoration

God created the heavens and the earth for His glory.

God made mankind in His image to fill the earth and subdue it.

This commission to mankind is known as the Dominion Mandate.

Mankind rebelled against God, bringing a curse upon all creation.

The curse brought suffering and death to the world; and made mankind's work burdensome.

The mandate to fill the earth and subdue it was reissued after The Fall.

God instituted a plan to restore mankind and all of creation.

Starting with Abraham, God chose a people who would be faithful to Him.

From this line came God's Son, Jesus Christ, who lived a life of perfect obedience.

Jesus was crucified and raised from the dead according to His Father's plan.

Jesus came not to condemn the world, but save it.

Jesus brings forgiveness and restoration to all who trust in Him.

Before ascending from the earth, Jesus issued the Great Commission as a resurrection of the Dominion Mandate to be fulfilled in His Name.

Those who trust Jesus are part of a new humanity that God is using to bring about a new creation.

Jesus now reigns at the right hand of the Father, overseeing the advance of His kingdom.

The Dominion Mandate is faithfully obeyed as God's people abide in Christ and serve others in His Name.

The day is coming when the earth will be filled with the knowledge of the Lord as the waters cover the sea.

Appendix B

A Prayer for Dominion

We praise you, O God, for all You have made.
> And we rejoice that You have called us to live in
> Your service.
> May the whole earth be filled and subdued for the
> glory of Your Name.

We confess to You, Father, we have not been faithful to
worship You and fulfill Your mandate.
> And we acknowledge how we have wasted Your gifts
> in unbelief.
> May You be pleased to forgive us and restore us
> with Your vision for the renewal of Your world.

We thank You, Jesus, for paying the price of our
redemption.
> And we present ourselves to You now as living
> sacrifices.
> May the gratitude we have for Your salvation always
> be with us, and compel us to pursue Your calling
> on our lives.

We ask You, Holy Spirit, to fill us with Your supernatural
power.
> And bring us the grace and truth we need to be
> those who serve faithfully.
> May You take our efforts and use them to advance
> the city of God, as we know our labor in the Lord is
> never in vain. Amen.

About the Author

David Bostrom has been helping people find their place in the world and use their God-given gifts for over 20 years.

For most of that time, David served as a church planter, pastor, counselor, and newspaper columnist. Currently, he assists individuals, entrepreneurs, publishers, professionals, and other leaders find their niche and implement their ideas through his copywriting and consulting services.

David is a Dan Kennedy Trained Copywriter for Info-Marketers. He is also an award winning writer from the highly regarded American Writers & Artists Inc.

He is available for writing projects, consultation, and speaking events.

David lives with his wife, Laura, in Central Florida, and he has six sons.

You can connect with David through his blog found at **madefordominion.com**.

DON'T STOP NOW!

STAY FOCUSED
AND
FULFILL YOUR PURPOSE

Get Ongoing Help From
madefordominion.com

This book was written to give you a start as you seek to find your purpose and live it. But it's only the beginning. Keep the journey going with regular inspiration and instruction from **madefordominion.com**.

At **madefordominion.com** you will receive:

- Ongoing reinforcement about God's purpose for your life, so you'll always know the "why" behind what you do.

- Stimulating ideas you can apply to live out your calling in the circumstances you face right now.

- Opportunities to receive further help to implement what YOU have to offer the world.

Visit **madefordominion.com** TODAY. While there, be sure and subscribe to the FREE *Made for Dominion* Newsletter, so you'll never miss the life-changing ideas you need to stay focused on your God-given purpose and fulfill it.

Visit madefordominion.com NOW